GW00726086

No. 204 is going home

A true story
of survival, love, motherhood and being human

By Marie Lindstrom

To Anton, Axel and Per.
For everything before, during, after and to come.
I love you.

November 2020

It's time.
Time to let this story travel the world.
I started to write this book in January 2005, and I guess I
needed this time to let it all mature before I was ready to let it
go, ready to give it wings of its own.
Now is the right time.
I know that.

This is not a Tsunami book – it's a book about being a human.
A book about losing yourself and finding yourself again. You,
but so very different.
It's about feeling as a failure as a parent when your children
needed you the most and to deal with that feeling of guilt.
It's a love story. About love for life. For family. For ourselves.
It's a story about forgiveness. It took some time for me to
forgive myself.
To forgive the panic attacks that hit me.
To forgive the ocean.

Most of all it's a story about being human.

Prolog

"I'm not afraid of anything, the worst has already happened".
The woman's gaze cuts through the television without asking
for permission. Her naked pain hits me right in my heart.
She lost her only child in a car accident in the 1980s and she
shares with the viewers that her grief has changed over the
years, but it never ever goes away. Time does not heal all
wounds, as they say.

Right then and there it hits me.
For the first time I understand.
Understand why I live in constant closeness to fear.
Because I have been in that place of darkness and chaos,
experiencing the worst thoughts and feelings running through
me. The place where I thought I had lost my children.
You never forget that feeling. It's boundless, bottomless,
devilish in its strength, life and mind changing like no other
feeling I've ever felt.
It has changed me as a mother and human being. My body, my
thoughts and my feelings. The way I look at myself and the
world.
Since the 26th of December 2004, I can imagine, not know,
that would be presumptuous, but imagine how life as we know
it can fall into pieces in seconds, and nothing will ever be the
same again.
Everything we know and cherish can be destroyed, life and
love as we know it turns into chaos, we find ourselves on the
verge of madness and hell.
That is why I am so scared. I am afraid of death, diseases,
drunk drivers, hurricanes, madness, the unexpected... that is
the worst... the unexpected... no control. No warning.
I fear anything and everything that could separate me from my
children. The love I have in my heart has a new
neighbor...fear.

It's not sound, not healthy, not intelligent, not realistic but very strong. Too strong for me to defend myself against.

As the woman continues to share her heartbreaking story, I also recognize myself in her description of feeling strong. How, after the loss of her daughter, without hesitation or asking for permission, she knows who she is, and she doesn't care about what people think of her.

The recognition is strong. In the middle of being the most fragile ever, eye to eye with the fragility of life, I have never felt stronger. I trust myself; I follow my intuition without any doubt, and from that strength I make quick undeniable decisions. I live life at a fast speed, spend my time wisely on well-chosen things and persons.

She helped me to understand what I have been struggling with - how I can be so afraid and fragile but at the same time stronger than ever before. Her words help me close the circle of questions and at that very moment I decide to finish writing my book. The book you are reading right now. The book I started to write the same day my children went back to school in January 2005.

I didn't return to work 100% until after summer 2005 as I needed to heal from the operations. So, I had plenty of time during the days to write.

This book is written from my memories, from my own perspective, no one else's, as my story is the only one, I can tell.

The story you are about to read involves my family: my husband Per and our two sons Anton and Axel. Axel was eight and Anton was eleven-years-old that day.

The book is about the unthinkable that might wait around the corner and how that affects life, and all our different roles in life.

The book is about the most important, strongest most valuable feelings of them all - love. It's also about darkness and survivor's guilt. Fear and feelings of not being enough.

How do you get over the feeling of guilt? Guilt as a survivor when others died? Guilt towards survivors that came home alone, without their relatives.

I feel an obligation to live my life fully, do as much good as I can for the ones, I have around me. To live nobly, fully present, to cherish the fact that I am one of those who survived.

But that is not easy. I find it difficult facing the surviving parents who were not as lucky as I was. Those that returned home without their children. The feeling that consumes me is related to shame and guilt. That feeling is unstoppable as it rushes through my body, as I want to bow in respect for their loss. I am so sorry... I wish there were something I could do, anything at all, that would help. But how can I ever ease your pain...

Please read my book straight through, as it is. The words are the ones that came to me, I cannot change them for fancier ones as they are naked and true, and the truth is what I want to share with you.

Nothing more, nothing less, nothing else.

This story is for you, who would like to understand what it is like to be thrown into something completely terrifying and sudden. Who want to get a glimpse of what it's like to lose your footing as a parent when you're most needed.

Try to feel the emotions as best you can and make something good out of it.

Read a little bit longer for your child tonight, give your mother an extra-long hug the next time you see her, rather say yes than no when someone asks for your help, listen carefully to your friends, smile to strangers, take care of and love yourself, enjoy the blue color of heaven, breath and make sure you listen to the birds...

Don't be afraid to make big changes in your life, always follow your gut feeling and your heart and don't live your life as if it will last forever. Because it will end one day.

Make the best of it until then.

5

The beginning

October 2003
Everything has a start. So does this story.

In October 2003 I visited a travel agency in Malmoe, Sweden.
My errand was to pick up a travel brochure about Thailand.
I will turn 40 on the 23rd of December 2004 and me and my
husband Per has decided to celebrate my birthday in Thailand.
It will be the first journey to Asia for our family.
I don't really know what I am looking for, but in the middle of
the brochure I find it - the picture I have dreamt of - a giant
blue pool surrounded by two lagoons and the most amazing
blue water - that's where we're going!
It feels so right!
The name of the hotel is Phi Phi Island Cabana and it is
located on Phi Phi Island.
We have decided to arrange the trip and book everything
ourselves, so this is the beginning of many hours of searching
for the islands and hotels to book for our three week vacation.
We make a lot of choices and changes during the planning, but
one thing remains the same no matter what – our stay at Phi
Phi Island Cabana.
Finally, everything is set: we have booked six different islands
and we are convinced that we have the vacation of our dreams
ahead of us.
We count down the days, when there is 103 days left, it feels
close.

My brother's dream

A week before our departure, my brother's girlfriend wakes up in the middle of the night. My brother is screaming out loud. His voice is filled with fear and he cries in despair.

His body is shaking as he shares his nightmare with her:

"I dreamed that Marie and I were walking along a stream.
The water is very current.
Suddenly Marie falls into the water and is dragged along by the swirls. It goes fast, terribly fast. I try to follow her, run on land along her side but I cannot keep up because she goes away with such speed in the water.
She approaches a bridge and there is ice covering the surface. She is pulled beneath the ice under the bridge.
I see her starting to swim like a seal, swimming up toward the ice, trying to break through the thick ice with her head so that she can breathe, get some air.
Her attempts get weaker and weaker and her efforts to break the ice fail. Suddenly it is still and quiet beneath the ice. I realize she is dead."

I was told about his dream a couple of weeks after we came home from Thailand. Still, I would not have changed anything if I knew about it.

As the day of departure is getting closer, we are all busy packing for the trip. Our living room floor is covered with bags and summer clothes. Toilet bags are filled with motion sickness tablets, Anton's asthma medicine, mosquito repellent, Advil and sunscreen.
Sune, our dog, will be staying with friends and relatives during our absence. His bag is also packed with food, candy, combs and his bed.

9

I don't sleep very well the night before our departure. I'm as enthusiastic as I was the night before Christmas Eve when I was a little girl.

December 17th, 2004 – the day of departure

We are all so excited that we wake up early.
It is so unreal, that we are having breakfast here in our kitchen and a couple of hours later, our journey to the other side of the world finally begins.
The children leave for school and we leave for work.
I have two important meetings and am well prepared. I put aside my thoughts of the trip and make sure I concentrate on my job. It's going to be a good day.
I close all the deals and it feels good.
I am happy and proud of my professional accomplishments this year and I do feel well deserved of a long, nice family vacation.
I wish all my colleagues a happy Christmas and run down to exchange money before I return home to meet up with the rest of my family.

They are already at home by the time I get there.
My father is also here, he will drive us to the central station.
After hugging my father goodbye, we head into the station and get on the train that will take us from Malmo to the airport in Copenhagen.

At last! Now the adventure finally begins!
Anton and Axel unpack their games and magazines. We point out that we may not have to unpack everything right now as this is only the short train journey across the bridge to the airport, Kastrup. That's when the big journey begins.

We check in our bags and go through security. It's Friday afternoon but not a lot of queues so after only one hour we stroll around the airport, in the search for a restaurant as we would like to have dinner before embarking the airplane. Anton has a lot of food allergies and even though I have informed the airlines, I don't rely on his food being enough and 100% safe for him to eat so I want him to embark the plane with a full stomach.

A Christmas choir passes us while we enjoy our dinner. The Christmas spirit fills the airport.

I love this.

Christmas is by far my favorite time of the year.

We arrive in Bangkok and have a three-hour slot before the flight to Krabi departs. It's exciting to just walk around in the airport. Everything is so different!

And from this moment, I start to collect and store the soft, warm, amazing scents of Thailand in my memory.

We find a Burger King close to our gate.

I would not have guessed that would be the first meal for us in Thailand, but it is and it tastes ok.

To be honest, I am in such a happy place mentally, they could have served me a chewing gum on a cucumber slice, and I would have rolled my eyes in pure joy.

The last hour before departure Per and I spend on the floor with our hand luggage as pillows and the children playing hide and seek around us, getting rid of some of the built-up energy from all the hours in the airplane.

The flight to Krabi is with Thai Air. Anton gets his allergy snacks and I am impressed. On all the flights from Kastrup to Krabi they have managed to secure food that he can eat. No eggs and no nuts, in any shape or form. And as language might be a problem in Thailand, I have his food allergies translated into Thai printed out to share with the restaurants we visit during our trip.

It's only a one-and-a-half-hour flight but we all fall deep asleep.

As we prepare for landing at Krabi airport, the view from the airplane surprises me. It's so beautiful, with a lot of hills and green nature. For some reason I expected a different kind of landscape, slightly burnt from the sun as this is the warmest period of the year in Thailand.

The airport is small, so we get our luggage as soon as we leave the airplane. The weather is changing fast. From blue sky and sunny to dark sky. The wind starts blowing and I can hear some thunder far away.

Outside the airport, in the parking lot across the street, men are lined up with signs with names written on them, I find our name and our driver right away. Isn't that amazing? I ordered a cab from our home in Sweden via Internet seven months ago and now it is here, right in front of me, in Thailand waiting for us.

He helps us with our luggage, and we start the forty-minute drive through villages and across fields.

The darkness falls upon us, in a few minutes it becomes totally dark. We leave the main street as he takes a left turn. The small road is bumpy. There are no houses, no lights. The driver makes a sharp turn and turns off the engine.

We leave the car and some young men help us with our luggage.

Our taxi drives away.

My eyes slowly get used to the darkness. I see a long, narrow pier going out into the ocean. A man waves to us from the far end. Hand in hand we walk in the warm humid air and the only thing that sounds is the men whispering in Thai and waves slowly rolling towards land.

My heart is pounding in my chest. Of excitement. Happiness. Love. Joy.

This is one of the most exciting things I've ever experienced.

"Kids, do you feel the scent? The scent of Thailand?"

I can't believe it's true, our journey has just started and it's already amazing.

"Mom, are we going on a boat now? Where is our boat?" whispers Axel, holding my hand.

"It's probably at the end of the pier."

A man helps us and our luggage into the boat. He starts the engine, and we leave land.
On our right side we see silhouettes of large, pointed cliffs. Even in darkness, the beauty is mind-blowing.
I close my eyes and take a deep breath, letting the scent fill me. Imagine that this is the scent of Thailand, how come no one ever mentioned that?
That Thailand has the most amazing aroma.

After fifteen minutes we turn right into a lagoon with high cliffs surrounding us.
Hotels scattered on the cliffs make beautiful clusters of lights. The boat drives up towards a beach and the driver signs for us to jump into the water and walk the last steps.
"Take off your shoes, we are going to walk in the ocean."
I don't have to ask twice. They pull of their shoes in pure excitement. I put the shoes in a bag, and we jump barefoot over the rail into the sea. Its lukewarm. Soft.
Our hotel is located on the other side of the cape and it will only take a few minutes to walk there.
We walk between huts and trees, it´s winding and very exciting.
When we arrive at our hotel Sand Sea Resort, the pool is the first thing we see, lovely blue and inviting. It´s allowed to swim in the pool until eight o'clock in the evening. It is seven o'clock now so in just a couple of minutes the kids have changed into their bathing suits and jumped into the pool.
Our bungalow is right beside the pool. I leave the front door open, enjoying the sound of them laughing and having fun as I unpack our bags.
Our bungalow is beautiful. A giant double bed for Per, me and Axel and an extra bed next to me for Anton.

We get ready for dinner and walk together barefoot along the beach. There are no cars here, the only sounds we hear are from the calm waves caressing the beach and people's laughter.

We have our first dinner in Thailand at a restaurant that will become a favorite we returned to several nights during our stay at Railay Beach. It is located on the beach, next to our hotel. The hotel owners are Muslim, so alcohol is sold at a bar down the beach. Per get us our very first Singa, Thai beer.
The menu is full of interesting choices, finally Per and I order a couple of Thai dishes to share and the children go for a classic: spaghetti Bolognese. The food turns out to be amazing. Anton even orders one more plate of spaghetti and empties that one as well.
Satisfied, full and slightly overwhelmed with the first couple of hours in Thailand we decide to return to our bungalow for a good night's sleep.
The children brush their teeth and crawl under the white crispy sheets. While I'm saying good night to them, Per turns on the Mp3 player and plugs in the travel speakers. We leave the front door open as we sit down for a while on our small porch.
"Can you believe we're here, Per? Twenty-four hours ago, we were at work, the kids at school and now we're sitting here!"
"Yes, isn't it amazing. And I really look forward to explore everything in daylight tomorrow."
We go to bed, Axel between us, Anton beside me.
We fall asleep right away.

December 19th, 2004

The next morning, Per wakes us up at nine o'clock.
I pull aside the curtains to let the sun in.
"Look!! Wow!! This is so beautiful! See the rock over there?
That's the one we could see last night when we came with the
boat."
We are surrounded by amazing nature, breathtaking cliffs and
incredible colors creating a view so beautiful that I just can't
get enough of it.
The children take some time to snuggle in bed while Per and I
get ready. I feel a little impatient. I want to leave the
bungalow. I want to go out and see, hear, walk, swim, run,
smell, feel...
"It's time to get up boys! We are off to breakfast. You can put
on your grey shorts and a t-shirt; you don't need shoes."
The breakfast tastes as lovely as it looks.
We got a table down by the beach overlooking the sea.
The omelette is unusually tasty, the coffee unusually good, the
melon juicier than I have ever tasted a melon before.
"Do you want to go to "the world's most beautiful beach"
today?" Per leans back in his chair, looking satisfied and
happy, gazing over the blue sea.
We have read that there is an amazing beach close to our hotel,
often referred to as breathtaking and very special.
"Yes! Let's do that! There was a sign over there showing the
direction. I think it's a ten minute walk, the beach is on the
other side of the cape."

The path to the beach is a beautiful stroll. A Thai woman
hanging her laundry smiles at us as we pass by.
After a curve, the path follows the mountain. Dripstone
formations are hanging over us. I hear a strange noise behind
me and turn around.
"Look kids! A monkey, a wild monkey!"

The kids eyes are the size of teacups as they gaze at the monkey, sitting on the roof of a small house, eating a banana. Looking at us as if Swedish tourist is an everyday occasion. "Per, we've only been here for fourteen hours and we've already experienced so many things."
He looks at me with a big smile, shaking his head in amusement. If I look anything like I feel, he's looking at a super happy Pippi Longstocking. On Christmas morning. That is how I feel anyway.

We walk around a cliff and the sky opens up and before us lays the most beautiful beach I have ever seen.
Wow, this must be "the world's most beautiful beach.
Imagine the most amazing blue sky, perfectly blue sea and white sand. In the horizon, giant cliffs in the ocean. Yes. This is the place we were supposed to find. I know that now. This will end up being the favorite beach during our week at Railey Beach.
We swim, play in the sand and enjoy the day. Lunch consists of fresh pineapple and grilled corn cobs sold on the beach, incredibly tasty!
Along the beach go vendors and before we leave the beach, we buy clothes for us all, comfortable Thai clothes in thin cotton. As the day turns into afternoon, we are all longing to get back to our hotel, to get a shower and put on some clothes to cover our skin from the sun.

We take a long-tail boat back to our hotel and when we are washed up wearing our new clothes, we jump on a long-tail boat into Ao Nang. The cash we had with us is running out and there is no ATM where we live. While in Ao Nang we are also buying snorkels and cyclops for the kids. And sandals.

In Ao Nang it's hot! Hot. Hot. Hot.
And crowded. There are cars everywhere, and everyone drives fast, you must run as fast as you can across the streets.
We do our errands without wasting any time and jump on a boat back to Railey Beach.

It feels so good to leave Ao Nang to return to our paradise where peace rules.

Dinner is as good as yesterday and after all the sunbathing and everything we've seen and been through we return to our bungalow at ten o'clock to put the children to bed.

Per and I finish our first day by just sitting on our terrace and lounging with a cold Singa in hand.

We decide to go to the world's most beautiful beach tomorrow as well and bring the cyclops and snorkels. It's going to be a good day!

The next two days we just relax, bathe, eat great food and enjoy ourselves.

Every night after dinner, we lie down on the beach and look at the stars. We do not go on any daytrips, we don't see any McDonald's, no shops.

We just relax and enjoy ourselves.

The evening of December 22nd, 2004

We have had dinner at the favorite restaurant every night so far. Seven different dishes as usual. Anton having his double serving of spaghetti Bolognese, as usual.
After dinner, we walk to the beach to lay down and watch the stars, as usual.
The sky is literally covered with thousands of stars. I have never ever seen a sky like this before.
As a lay there, it hits me. I can't remember the last time I felt this happy. So at peace, as right here, right now. Time stands still and I can feel my body being more and more relaxed and heavy in the most pleasant of ways.

Barefoot hand in hand we walk back towards our bungalow along the beach. We pass the beautiful, illuminated pool and walk into our bungalow.
Anton and Axel fall asleep at the same time as their heads touch the soft pillow. I understand why. They are having so much fun, from the moment they wake up until the moment they go to bed. The only time they are still is during our meals.

The air is nice and warm, so we decide to play a game of cards and share a Singa out on our porch before we go to bed.
Per wins - unfortunately.
"So, my dear, you actually turn forty right now here in Thailand. How does it feel?" He leans over the table and gives me a kiss.
"Except that I'm obviously lousy at this game of cards, I have to say life is pretty great. But turning forty might not be as fun as it was turning thirty, or thirty-five."
"If you live to eighty, you'll have half your life left."
"Thank you for that. No, but honestly, if you're happy with how your life has turned out, with the person you have become, I guess any birthday is a nice birthday? Right?" I smile at him.

My mobile phone beeps. It's a text from dad. I'm impressed
that he has track over time here in Thailand as he is on
vacation in Florida.
"What does he write?"
I read aloud.
"Dear Marie, I wish you a really nice birthday over there, in
the other part of the world. I'm thinking about you. I love you.
Hugs from your father & Lena"

We go to bed hand in hand next to a sleeping Axel in the giant
double bed. Anton sleeps in his bed next to me.
So, I'm forty years old now....

My father's first dream

My father and his spouse Lena are on vacation in Florida,
visiting close friends. He wakes her up in the middle of the
night to share his nightmare.
His voice is filled with fear and desperation.

*"Anton and I are on a beach surrounded by a bay. In the
middle of the bay there is a lighthouse, it is very high. Along
the lighthouse there are stairs that wind up to the top. I see
Anton running up along the stairs and I try to yell at him to
come down because it looks dangerous. He doesn't hear me.
He continues up. Suddenly, when he approaches the top, he
loses his footing and falls! I see his body falling from the high
altitude, towards the rock cliffs below, pointed and lethal. I'm
screaming straight out. When his body is close to the rocks, a
gust of wind comes and grabs his body and brings it out to
the sea and he is rescued."*

My father sends me a text the next day:
"Marie, DON'T let Anton climb anywhere high.
Hugs Dad"

I never got that text.

December 23rd, 2004 – my birthday

They wake me up at eight o'clock.
The mp3 player plays the "Happy birthday" song by the Smurfs on high volume. Anton and Axel jump into my bed and Per opens a bottle of champagne.
I have received many text messages during the night. From my mom, friends and my brother's family. I read the messages while Per pours the champagne into two glasses.
"Happy birthday!"
"Have a really lovely birthday over there in Paradise. Love from us back home in dark cold Sweden..."
"Dear sister, congratulations on the 40th anniversary wishes P-O, Bryndis, Ellen & Erik"

I get a boat trip as a birthday present from Per. We are going on an all-day island jumping with a speedboat.
With a glass of champagne in my hand, I stroll around in our large, beautiful bungalow. I open the door to take a glance at the pool and the ocean behind it, between the palm trees. I take a deep breath, feel how the morning air fills my lungs. Anton joins me on the porch, as he's filming our bungalow with our video camera in his hand.
"And here we have the pool", he says into the camera.
"And here we have your mom", I say and make a funny face into the camera. "Do you see how blue the sea is today? In an hour, we are going to go out to Chicken Island and snorkel. Is it going to be fun?"
"Are we going to snorkel in deep water? Really, really deep Mom?"
"No, I don't think so. And we are all going to have life jackets so it's going to be easy to be completely still in the water, just floating on the surface without moving."

The speed boat has four staff members taking care of us seven passengers. It's our family, a young American couple and an older woman from South America.

Our first stop is outside a beautiful island. We lay anchor and prepare to jump in. I look into the clear water, not a fish in sight.

"Per, there are no fish in the ocean?"

At the same time, they throw bread into the water and the sea is suddenly boiling with hundreds of yellow, green and blue fantasy fish. It's amazing. And a little creepy as we can feel them against us.

It's like being part of a Disney movie.

After an hour, we leave for our next destination, Chicken Island.

The boat anchors in the middle of two islands, it's just a tiny strip of beach that connects the two islands. I stand there, with closed eyes, and breathe.

It feels like I'm standing in the middle of the universe.

As I return to the others, I can hear my mobile phone from my bag. It's my best friend Anette wanting to congratulate me on my birthday. She is also in Florida on vacation, just like my dad.

It's so strange to hear her familiar voice while I look out over the island.

Right now, we are on different sides of the globe. So close, yet so far apart at the same time.

The boat trip is coming to an end and we ask them to leave us at the world's most beautiful beach.

We stroll back to our hotel, enjoying every minute. Back at the hotel the kids play in the pool as Per and I get ready for my birthday dinner.

We pack everyone's luggage so that everything is prepared for our journey to Phi Phi Island tomorrow morning.

Per and the children have reserved our favorite table at our favorite restaurant. By now we don´t even have to take a look at the menu.

Per and I order some of the hot Thai dishes while the children run their safe card in replay even tonight, spaghetti Bolognese.

After dinner we walk barefoot to the bar on the beach.

Anton has gone ahead and is waiting for us at a nice spot on the beach that he picked out for us.

"Here's a good spot Mom, right?"

"Absolutely perfect, Anton, it can't get any better."

Per comes back from the bar with two cold gin and tonic and Coke for the kids.

Hand in hand, on our back, looking at the sky full of stars and the moon. Some soft music from a bar. We chat and just enjoy each other's company.

A beautiful day at Railey Beach comes to an end.

So does my 40th birthday.

Christmas Eve

We enjoy our last breakfast at Railey Beach.
It's a little sad to leave. We've had such an amazing time here.
Our expectations have been more than met.
We have put our luggage by the front door of the bungalow
and the boat leaves in an hour.
Per and I go to the reception to pay the restaurant bills and
take the opportunity to ask them about Christmas next year.
Because we want to come back, we both feel that.
The woman at the reception tells us that we must wait a couple
of months before we can make reservations for next year, so
we have to email the hotel later on.
We book one more night though– the last night before we'll fly
back to Bangkok, after we traveled around the islands. We
were going to stay in Krabi that night, close to the airport. But
we have changed our mind, we want to sleep here one last
night.
The night between the 4th and 5th of January.

A long-tail boat picks us up at the beach to take us out to the
big boat anchored further out on deep water. That's the boat
that will take us to Phi Phi Island.
It's a really hot day so we choose to sit inside the boat where
there's air conditioning. The trip will take about 90 minutes.
In front of us on the wall, is a map of Thailand. We point out
all the islands we are going to visit for the kids.
They play with their game boys and I take the opportunity to
send Christmas greetings text messages to friends and family.
I just learned how to add recipients, so almost every contact I
have got my text:
*"Today we left Railey Beach, a true paradise on earth, to
celebrate Christmas Eve on Phi Phi Island.
We will leave Phi Phi Island for Koh Lanta on the 27th of
December.
We wish you all a lovely Christmas!
Many hugs from the four of us to you."*

The boat approaches Phi Phi Island.
We are staying at a big fancy hotel and tonight we will have
Christmas dinner there. It's going to be a lot of people and lots
of good food.
"Will there be a Santa Claus at the party?"
"I don't know for sure Axel, but I guess he will come by if he's
not too busy."
"Do you think all children are going to get Christmas presents?
You know, that flute we saw on the beach last night, maybe I'll
get that from Santa?"
"Maybe Axel, fingers crossed." I smile at him. I bought the
flute yesterday and packed it in our luggage.
We go ashore and at the same second our feet touch Phi Phi
Island, the air is filled with stress.
It's crowded around us and the air is hot.
It does not feel at all like Railey Beach. Rather the opposite.
People are screaming about boat rental, rooms to rent...
"Ugh, I don't like it here Per. It's really stressful..."
"I know, but I'm sure it is going to be fine. I think it's just
chaotic here where everyone comes ashore." He looks around.
"Where is our hotel?"
"It should be here nearby" As I lift my head up, I realize we are
standing right in front of our hotel, Phi Phi Island Cabana.
The reception area is huge, jet quiet. The scent is luxurious,
walls and floor in marble. A young woman from Holland, or a
nearby country, takes care of us.
"We need to have a deposit. Either a copy of your Visa or your
passport."
She gets my passport as a deposit, and we fill out various
papers with our names and address.
A friendly man assists us with our luggage.
The room is located on the third floor in the annex to the left
of the main building. The room gets a bit crowded with three
beds, as we've asked for an extra bed for Anton, but the view is
amazing. Through the huge terrace doors, we can see the
entire bay on the other side of the island.

I don't know what's happening to us.

It's like someone's put a big grey blanket all over us. As we fell into a deep hole here on Phi Phi. We're restless and don't know what to do.

Down by the pool that I've dreamed of for so long, the reason we are here, all the chairs are taken. There's no place for us there. We take a swim but have nowhere to sit afterwards. So, we decide to go down to the beach. The sand at the beach is full of shards of glass.

It does not feel good to be here.

At all.

If we had not already prepaid three nights at the hotel, I would have taken my family and left Phi Phi Island first thing the next morning.

Just leave, as I realize my Phi Phi Island fantasy, was exactly that – a fantasy. Reality is nothing like I expected it to be. Or wanted for my family.

"Let's go to the room and relax." Per is the only one of us that is in a reasonably good mood and he is doing his best to cheer us all up.

"We're hungry." Anton and Axel both look saggy and tired.

"All the restaurants at our hotel are closed as the staff are busy preparing for the Christmas party tonight. But mom and I can go into the village and get you something to eat. You can hang out in the room, take a nap or play game boy in the meantime. Okay?"

They don't need any convincing, a couple of minutes later they are tucked in, looking very cozy, both playing with their game boy.

Per and I find the small street through the village. Shops and small restaurants side by side. We get Anton a Christmas gift, some food, and drinks.

One and a half hour later we are back at our hotel

The key to our room must be put in a socket in the wall to get electricity in the room so we don't have a key. We need them to open the door for us.

I knock on the door.

No one opens, there's not a sound from the room.

We knock a little harder.

"Anton and Axel, please open the door!"

Still not a sound from the room. I am getting worried.
What if they have left the room? What if they've gone to the pool? Where are they?
Suddenly I hear a noise from the stairs below us. It's one of the staff members of the hotel. I run down to him and explain that we are locked out of our room, and asked if he could please help us?
He opens our door.
There they are.
Our two children.
Totally knocked out.
So peaceful. Side by side in the huge bed.
Phew... that was a scary couple of minutes, thinking they were not here...
We look at them, game boys in hand, safe and sound asleep. They are exhausted. I'm so happy they get some rest so that they can enjoy the party tonight.
We decide to enjoy some bruschetta with mozzarella out on our balcony.
The view is beautiful, there's no doubt about that. But I don't get the tingling feeling I got at Railey beach. I'm not touched by the nature nor the atmosphere.
When we've finished our bruschetta, we call our family members in Sweden and my dad in Florida, wishing everyone a Merry Christmas.

The conversation with my father is strange.
"Don't you regret it, Marie?"
He's not been positive about us taking this trip for some reason.
"Dad, I've just told you about our amazing week at Railey Beach. Of course, we don't regret this trip. Why would we?"
"Did you get my text about Anton?"
"No, what text about Anton?"
"I had such a strange dream. A nightmare about Anton and a high lighthouse. From the top of the lighthouse he fell towards the sharp cliffs beneath him. At the very last moment he was rescued by a gust of wind. Marie don't let him climb anywhere high. That goes for Axel to."

"Ok. I promise, Dad, none of them will be allowed to climb any heights."

My father does not usually sound like this; it's out of his character to say things like this. It makes me very uncomfortable. I cannot ignore what he just said, he sounds too concerned for me to do that. I don't know how to handle the information. I shudder.

"I promise, Dad, I will not let them climb high."

We say goodbye with lots of hugs and a promise to talk again soon.

My mother is spending Christmas at my brother's house. They are in the middle of the Christmas celebration when I call them.

It does feel strange not to be with our family today, on Christmas Eve.

The children wake up after a while. We serve them some buns and juice as we start to get ready for dinner. This is the first night we put on some nice clothes here in Thailand.

As we walk from our room and annex towards the huge open space in front of the main building where the party is, we realize how many guests there are at this hotel. Several hundred I would guess.

I understand why the staff were busy preparing all day.

It's absolutely amazing. So beautiful! Flower arrangements, Christmas light in the trees. Orchids everywhere. Light loops that shine above us in the dark. A scene with a painted Santa Claus. I'm guessing we're up to five or six hundred guests at the party.

The buffe is huge. From sushi to melons carved into pieces of art, water chestnuts, grilled lobster. And it tastes amazing.

Anton and Axel get some food but as soon as they find the ice cream buffe, they set their focus on that instead of food.

And I let them.

Its only Christmas once a year.

Up on the stage, there's entertainment all night long. Thai boxing, funny competitions, singing and music. With magnificent fireworks lighting up the sky, a beautiful Christmas Eve party comes to an end.

We fall asleep as soon as our heads touch the pillows.

December 25th, 2004

"Good morning! Time to get up! We're going snorkeling today." Per is an early riser as usual. "I let you sleep in, but now you really have to get up. We missed breakfast at the hotel, they stopped serving half an hour ago, but I thought we could get some buns and juice and bring on to the boat. It leaves in forty-five minutes. Make sure you do not forget to bring your snorkels and cyclops. And bring some extra clothes. We won't be back until tonight."

Our hotel has arranged a full day trip for the hotel guests. The boat is large, there's a lot of space as we only are ten passengers. Our family, a Dutch family and a Japanese couple. We visit different places and islands. Bamboo island being one of them, a lovely place with lots of monkeys.

The trip back to the hotel is peaceful.

We lay side by side on the deck, the sun has begun to set, coloring the sky pink.

"What a day!" Per looks satisfied and very relaxed. "We have settled in here now, Marie. You'll see, the rest of our days here at Phi Phi are going to be great!"

"I agree. It does feel much better now. Where do you think we should have dinner tonight, in the village maybe?"

"Maybe? Let's take a stroll into the village and see where we end up?"

In the village most restaurants are already full. Or have reservations for the whole night.

We return to our hotel and get a table at one of the restaurants down by the beach. It's really cozy. You can even sit directly in the sand, with low tables and on pillows instead of chairs.

Unfortunately, those tables are reserved for tonight, so we get an ordinary table but make sure that we have a reservation down at the beach for tomorrow night.

The 26th of December.

My father's dream on the night of December 26th.

My father is screaming out loud, waking up Lena.
He's terrified and all sweaty.
Lena gets out of bed and he shares his nightmare with her.

"I'm on the ground floor of this multi-level building where we live right now in Florida. It's an open garage with no walls. A giant black cobra, a snake, is following me. The snake raises up high above me. It has got a sealed face and it's attacking me. I manage to escape the first two attacks, I try to run away from it, but the snake is following me. Its hovering over me. High, wide face, black.
I gaze up. Suddenly it attacks me from above. I just scream......
It's like a big black wave rolling over me."

December 26th, 2004

We wake up at half past eight.
I stay in bed for a while, cuddling up with Per´s arms around me.
I look around our room. It is going to be nice to leave tomorrow, Phi Phi Island was not my Island. I knew that from the first step I took on this island. I can't wait to leave. I long for the rest of our trip to begin.
"What do you want to do today Per? Relax by the pool?"
"I would like to go to Long Beach and see if Mia and Klas have arrived. I heard that's a really nice part of this island. That's probably where we should have stayed instead of here, right in the middle of everything." Mia and Klas are some friends from Malmo.
I turn around and wrap my legs around his. "Then I suggest we stay here and swim in the pool, have some lunch and after that we could take a long-tail boat to Long Beach early afternoon."
Given that all the sun beds were occupied on the day we arrived, Per decides to go down and make sure we have some chairs today by reserving them.
"Where would you like to be?"
"Hmm..take two chairs between the pool and the beach."
"Okay, I'll take care of it. Could you make sure you and the kids are ready to go when I get back? So that we can get some breakfast right away."
"Yes, we are about to get up now.... "
The bed is so comfortable that I could have stayed there for a while longer. I smile at him as he turns around before the door closes behind him.
I decide to stay in bed just a little bit longer...
"Mom, what are we going to do today?" Anton is awake.
"We'll stay here at the hotel and then we'll have lunch before taking a long-tail to Long Beach. Does that sound like a good plan to you?"
"Mmmmm"

The children remain in their beds and play Game Boy for a while longer. I let my eyes glaze over them. They are getting a nice tan. No one's got sunburned. That's good.
Per's returning to the room.
"Aren't you ready to go?? What a lazy family I've got! Make sure to get ready now or we are going to miss breakfast."
I smile, I love that he is our wake-up alarm.

Suddenly I feel my bed starting to shake.
Clear lateral shaking.
Not fast, but rather slow.
But very noticeable.
"Per, do you feel that?"
"Feel what?" He walks up to my bed where I'm still under the cover.
"The bed, and I, are shaking?"
It sounds like a question, but it's not. I know it's shaking. I can feel it clearly. But the sensation is so surreal that I hardly trust my own feeling.
Per puts his hand on my hip. I try to convince him, it's so obvious to me.
"Honestly Per? What is this? Why is it shaking?"
"I don't feel anything?"
"The entire bed is shaking. Don't you sense it?"
No, he does not. The shaking stops and I understand that I won't get any explanation.
Maybe I was imagining it all?
But... no... my bed did shake... didn't it?
I get up from bed, put on my newly bought Thai clothes, put sunscreen on the kids while I enjoy the view through the windows towards the bay.
The ocean and the sky are blue, not a cloud in sight.
It is going to be an amazing day.

Quarter to nine, we're finally ready to leave the room.
"Did you bring the breakfast tickets, Per?" He nods. "Let's go back to the room after we have had our breakfast to get our bathing stuff, right?"

Hand in hand we stroll to the main building where breakfast is served.

This is our second day here at Phi Phi Island. As we were out on a snorkeling excursion yesterday, this is our first breakfast at the hotel.

Per took the opportunity to check the range of food on the buffet while he was out by the pool earlier, so he guides us around.

"There's omelet over there, pineapple, melon and lots of different cereals over here."

We get a table for four, next to a French family with three kids. Everyone is having breakfast except the mother. She drinks coffee and smokes cigarette after cigarette. I look at her when Anton gets the smoke from her cigarette in his face for the third time in a couple of minutes.

She looks at me, fiddles the cigarette and lights a new one.

We take turns to go and get food, Anton's plate is filled with pineapples and melons. Axel fancies the part of the breakfast buffet that contains sausages and bacon.

After a third cup of coffee we are satisfied and leave the restaurant to go to our room and get the things we want to bring to the pool.

We arrive to our sun lounges, between the pool and the beach, around ten o'clock.

My feet are red and bloated from mosquitoes and it hurts. I can't even put my feet into my sandals. We went to a pharmacy yesterday and bought a cortisone ointment that would help with the swelling and although it eased a bit, it still stings badly in the sun.

Per aims for the reception to ask if there is a doctor in the hotel, it might be good to have a dose of antibiotics to be able to get into a pair of shoes again. Not least considering that tomorrow we will continue our journey, leaving for Koh Lanta where we have friends waiting for us.

"I will ask about a doctor and I will also see if I can find something to read. Do you need anything?"

"No, but please ask if we can book tickets for the boat tomorrow? And also check if there is a boat that leaves before 2pm? I'd like to leave Phi Phi Island already in the morning if possible."

The sunlounges next to us are facing the sea but ours are facing the pool, which is good so that I can keep an eye on our kids playing in the pool.

The pool has the shape of three large circles. The circles have different depths, and the kids are in the children's pool on the far right from where I am

On the other side of the pool, opposite to me, is the hotel's main building where we had breakfast. There are annex buildings on both side of the main building. All buildings have four floors. The hotel covers the entire area between the two bays. It is a nice hotel, built of stone and concrete and surrounded by palm trees.

On my left side is a woman in her fifties.

She's facing the bay behind me, fully focused on reading her book. On my right side is a young couple who are also reading. Other than them, it is quite empty around the pool so far, it's still early in the day.

I settle down as Per leaves for his errands.

My feet really hurt in the sunlight.

I try to use the beach towel to protect them, but it doesn't work very well.

Anton and Axel have put the floating football goals into the children's pool.

Axel comes running to me." Mom, we need our ball because we're going to play with the goals. May I have our room key?"

"Axel, while you're going up to our room, could you please also bring me a small towel from our bathroom. I will soak it in cold water and cover my feet with it."

"What size should the towel be?" He really wants to bring me the exact right towel.

"Not the smallest, but one that is like this." I show him the approximate size with my hands.

Axel ponders for a few seconds about the size and disappears towards the annex and our room.

I lean back and close my eyes. After a little while I open my eyes because I notice that the woman to my left is moving. She stands up now.

I glance at her from my sun lounger. She is covering her eyes from the sun as she gazes over the bay. The beach is right below us. There is just a garden bed between the pool and the beach, some gardeners are taking care of the flowers right next to us.

There is something with the way the woman next to me looks out over the ocean that makes me want to get up from my chair.

I just get the urge to see what she's looking at, so I do the same as she does.

At first, I don´t understand what we are looking at but after a few minutes I see a surge that looms in the lagoon. The lagoon has the shape of a horseshoe. The wave is visible in the small gap.

The sky is still clear blue.

There is no wind.

The sun is large and bright.

It's a beautiful day in Thailand.

Right in front of us in the ocean, a beautiful young woman walks towards the beach. She's been swimming further out, I guess. It's incredibly shallow in the bay, even though she's pretty far out, the water only reaches her knees.

Per returns from his stroll.

"Look at the wave, can you get it on video? Should we get the kids to watch?"

"There is no doctor at our hotel, but if we need help, the hospital is right next door", Per says as he picks up the video camera from his backpack and starts filming. He's standing right behind me.

I continue to look at the woman who is walking towards the beach.

She's stunningly beautiful, she would fit perfectly into a scene in a Bond movie.

Further out in the bay, I can see a speedboat. The driver tries to turn the boat to face the wave instead of being hit by the side. Just before the wave reaches the boat, it seems like the water is "sucked up" beneath it. The man loses control of his boat. The next second, the wave grabs the boat from the side and with a terrible speed, the boat travels sideways towards the beach.

Now, alarm bells go off inside me.

The gardener in the flower bed below me begin to wave towards the people that are still in the ocean to hurry up.

No one is screaming. They just wave.

The beautiful woman starts to walk a little faster, almost run. But she is still far out, maybe sixty-five feet away from us.

An accident is going to happen.

Someone is going to get hit by a boat!

Chaotic thoughts go through my mind as I turn my head to the left side of the bay. There is a long-tail boat that also moves sideways in high speed towards the beach. In the water in front of the boat, is a man. All I can see is his head, so I think that he just fell.

In retrospective, I know that the level of the ocean is at least ten feet higher than normal. But that never crosses my mind. I don´t understand what I see because my mind sets up limits of what is realistic, possible, believable, and likely.

I have never heard about what we are going to be part of in just a couple of seconds. I didn't know this could happen.

I have no clue what's going on in front of us.

"The boat will run him over!" I'm screaming to Per standing behind me, still filming.

The woman and the couple who was next to me must have run away. I don't see them anymore.

Our camera, Anton's allergy medicine, my phone and other important items are in my backpack. I want to hurry back to my sun lounger to fetch it, to protect it from water splashing up from the ocean.

As I quickly move towards the sun loungers, I can see the ground in front of me.

I bend over to pick up the backpack.

Suddenly it's neither hot nor cold in the air, I don't hear any sounds and I'm not thinking any thoughts.

My heart is beating so hard that I can feel it in my entire body. I don't know where Anton and Axel are and I don't know, don't understand, what's going on...

All I know is that we are surrounded by danger, a danger much larger than anything my brain could possibly imagine.

I'm not afraid, it's worse than that.

I'm terrified.

I turn around and head towards the children's pool.

The big pool is to my left side and I have the ocean on my right side as I move forward. The "aisle" in between is about 10 feet wide.

As I start walking, in one second, I am suddenly walking in knee-high brownish-grey water.

In the swirling water, sun loungers unexpectedly start to float around.

As I continue to move forward as fast as I can, I need to push the sun loungers away as they are being thrown really hard against my legs due to the heavy swirls in the dark water.

I have my backpack in my left hand and can only protect myself from the chairs with my right hand.

I'm not thinking anything.

I panic, everything is completely unreal; this is not happening, I'm not here, this is not true!

WHERE ARE MY CHILDREN?????

I don't know how many steps I've managed to walk. My view is locked towards the ground, on the grey dark swirling water that surrounds me.

I don't look up as I try to move forward as fast as I can.

I scream from the top of my lounges to Per: "Take care of the kids!!"

Without raising my head, without looking at him. I don't even know where he is, but I believe he's somewhere behind me.

The water is so dirty and swirly, it's impossible to see the ground under my feet.

I try to move as fast as possible to get to the children's pool where I think, where I'm convinced my sons must be...

Suddenly I'm falling. To my left, towards the pool.

As I can't see the ground through the dark water, I've walked straight towards the pool instead of alongside it.
With my left foot, I take a step into the deep end of the pool.
In what feels like slow motion, I'm falling into the pool where the blue water quickly mixes with the filthy swirling ocean that by now has raised up on land. With violence, speed and evil force it's taking over everything in its path.
I lift my head as I fall.
A young man is approaching, he is running towards the main building, away from the beach.
His path is crossing mine but he's a couple of feet in front of me.
He looks straight at me, our eyes meet.
With full speed he starts to run towards me instead of continuing his own path, towards his safety.
He is in front of me in a second.
With his left hand he grabs my right hand with a firm grip.
With the other hand he rips the backpack out of my hand and as in slow-motion I see it flying high up in the air. I don't understand why he's throwing it away.
I need to protect Anton's medicine.
I feel his firm grip.
I feel how I fall...
After that, all is dark.

In the grip of the Tsunami

Everything is dark around me.
Or do I have my eyes closed?
I don't know.
I really don't know.
I feel my body spinning around, swirling around at a very high speed.
In my body, my stomach, it feels like I am in a hysterical carousel.
I am completely powerless.
My body is out of my control.
I don't protect myself.
I don't keep my arms and legs close to my body.
Everything is happening so fast. The speed is lethal.
I have no thoughts.
I only have feelings. Resignation, paralysis, horror and complete unreality.
I don't have any time perspective.
I don't feel like I'm drowning.
Everything inside me is paralyzed as my body is tossed around at a speed that is so frighteningly high, swirls and currents so strong that nothing can escape them.
I'm not thinking that I'm going to die, but I do give up after a while.
I have no choice.
I surrender.
Death does not scare me.
Death cannot be more terrifying than what's happening right now.
It's hard to put words to it.
My body is in a ready to fight mood, prepared but still paralyzed.

Suddenly, I don't know after how long, I "wake up".
I've started treading water before I knew what I was doing.

I'm in deep water, I cannot reach the bottom.
It is completely pitch-dark around me.
It is completely silent.
The contrast from the sun and blue sky is massive.
I have concrete towards my head.
I can only get my nose above the surface of the water; my
mouth is below due to the narrow gap between the water and
the concrete.
The space between the water and the concrete over my head is
only 6 inches.
My breathing is terribly fast, short breaths through my nose.

I see the contour of my grandmother's face in front of me.
Trying to feel her strength, the security she has signified to me.
She does not derive by herself – I force her image to develop in
front of me.
My first feeling is that the children must have made it, that
they must be in safety.
The first thought is "No one will look for me here..."
I instinctively know that I'm in a very strange place.
A place you should not be in.
A place where no one's going to look for me.
Then an insight hit me: I need to breathe slowly, otherwise the
air in this narrow space will run out.
GOD!!
I'm just an ordinary mother. I don't know anything about this!
I'm more scared than I've ever been, I'm in my worst
imaginable nightmare.

After a few seconds in the darkness I discover that I am not
alone, there is a person next to me.
I cannot see anything, but I feel it.
My grandmother's image disappears before me. My brain
starts working. I get 100% focused.
It feels like we are trapped in a square meter of concrete both
over us and around us.
I have no idea where we are or how we ended up here.
I don't know who's next to me.
I grab a hand. Or was I holding on to it already?

I don't know.

My grip is terribly hard; it must hurt.

"Don't leave me here..." I whisper in English, leaning my head backwards to get my mouth above the water. My words are mixed with a gurgling sound as water comes into my mouth.

I don't know why I speak English.

One thing I know is that I don't have any bikini bottom on, the hard currents in the wave ripped them away. I know that I am naked except for my bikini top.

Gurgling in English, I say to the person next to me. "I'm not wearing any pants."

Not that it's important.

I don't even know why I'm saying that.

Everything is so unreal!

A while ago I was in paradise with my husband and children. Then suddenly I am fighting for my life in current deep water and now I am in another terrifying scene in this horror movie that I have never asked to be part of.

Stuck in pitch black darkness, underground in deep water up to my nose, almost naked with an unknown man beside me. I don't get an instinct for survival, on the contrary, the fear of not getting through this alive is overwhelming. My mind is paralyzed, at the same time as I'm fighting to keep myself from panicking.

"I think I know where we need to go", says the man by my side gurgling as water comes into his mouth.

I have no idea where we are, no idea which way we should go, so I let him take command.

Suddenly I sense he's doing something with his hand. I can't see what it is, but being so close to him in the darkness, I instinctively, without thinking, start to do what I believe he is doing. I don't realize what I'm doing until I've already done it – I've put my arm under one of the concrete beams that surround us from the ceiling. That's how we realize that we are not surrounded by walls, but by beams from the ceiling over our head. The beams come down from the ceiling by about 15 inches.

We stretch as much as we can to reach around.

Desperately searching for air pockets on the other side, to find out if it's even possible to dive beneath the beams, from air pocket to air pocket.

The water level isn't changing. It's not getting any lower.
We keep on tilting our heads backward to breath, to get air.
"We have to dive," he says.
He takes a deep breath, and he starts diving down through the water.
Without hesitation, I take a deep breath and dive after him, keeping my firm grip around his hand, my lifeline.
As we reach the next air pocket, still pitch black, I get a feeling the air pocket is smaller. I need to tilt my head even more backwards to get air.
Everything is happening so fast. That's probably for the best, as the panic starts to raise within me, and I know this is not the time or place to lose control.
I'm going to die here if I don't concentrate on surviving and moving forward.
We continue to use our arms beneath the beams in the search for air pockets in the next box. We do this diving from box to box. Moving as fast as we can in silence.
We don't speak another word to each other.
Suddenly, as I get to the surface in a box, my hand is empty.
I'm alone – he's gone!
I'm alone!!
The only thing that should not happen, wasn't supposed to happen, just happened.
I'm all alone in the darkness.
Surrounded by concrete and water and I am terrified.
I don't want to die, not here, not now, not this way...

Somehow, I get hold of myself. I do not give up.
I will not let panic paralyze me.
I take the deepest breath of my life and dive deep down in the water.
It suddenly feels different, maybe because I'm alone.
Maybe because I'm so scared.

I dive further than before, with heavier strokes, further down in the deep water.
Everything goes fast.
I swim for my life.
I swim either in the right direction... or in the wrong direction...
When I reach the surface, I find myself in some kind of pipe.
Suddenly I see a beam of light on my right side.
I will survive!
I will survive.

The man whose hand I was holding, my lifeline, sits further ahead in the pipe.
The water is high and filled with debris.
He is hurt.
I see him from behind as he sits there, bent over in a strange angle, trying to hold up his right arm and shoulder.
He breathes heavily, he is in a lot of pain.
The pipe is about 10 feet long, filled with water and debris. I just know that he's not able to move towards the opening by himself.
I move around him so that I can push away large pieces of wood and debris.
As soon as I have managed to make more room for him, I push him forward.
Move debris, push him.
Move debris, push him.
I don't know how long it takes.
We don't say anything to each other. We don't see each other's faces.
After a while, we finally reach the end of the pipe. There is a sideways staircase, but it's jammed by floating things.
Eventually he manages to make his way up.
I see him disappear.
Am I still in deep water?
I don't know, I really don't know.
But I do know that I have to struggle and fight some more before I can reach the stairs.
I don't know how I got up from the pipe.

When I finally manage to leave the underground, I realize that I am at the pool area, where I was when the Tsunami took me. My body weights a ton.

I´m exhausted, I´m tired, but I feel no pain.

The sun shines so vibrant from the clear blue sky.

There is nobody here.

The only thing I see is broken sun loungers, debris, and chaos.

It's quiet.

Not a sound.

I don't know what happened here while I was underground.

I have not jet understood that the wave that hit land was not a wave. It was several miles of ocean, masses of water that just came and came, that the water level was about 23 to 26 feet high.

When I "woke up" underground, the sea level was at least 13 or 14 feet above my head.

I look around, dazzled by the sun after being in darkness so long.

I search for something to wrap around my hips, as I have lost my bikini pants. Next to me on the ground, I find part of a plastic beach parasol. White and green, covered with a thick layer of wet clay.

I bend over and pick it up, it's rough and dirty, but it will do.

As I wrap it around me, the parts of the plastic sheet meet at my right hip. I look down and see a round hole, the size of an apple, in my flesh at the hip bone.

I look right into my own flesh. There is no blood flowing.

Inside the flesh, it does not look like I would have thought it to be, tendons and stuff, but small beige-red "bubbles" embedded in red meat.

I start walking along the pool towards the main building. I am heading to our annex, the only thought I have is to go straight to our room, there's nothing else in my mind.

Per, Anton and Axel are there, waiting for me. In my mind, this has only hit me and the man I met. No one else. Especially not my children.

Once again, my brain sets limits to what is possible.

As I take my third step I scream as loud as I can "Per, Anton, Axel!!"
Just in case they are not in our room.
I'm not screaming in panic; I'm just screaming as loud as I can.
No one is answering.
What I don't know is that Per can hear me calling for him, but he can't answer me.
He is stuck underground in an air space treading water.
He is surrounded by darkness and water just like I was until now.
When he hears me, he thinks, "Marie has made it, so will I."

It's a long way to our annex, you must follow a winding path.
I walk fast, but I don't run.
It's completely empty, not a human being around me.
As I approach our building, I look up at the loft aisle along our floor.
There I see Axel on the 4th floor out on the loft aisle, facing me.
He stands there, eight years old.
I can only see his face, it´s white.
He is all alone.
He looks down, turn his head my direction and sees me.
He screams from the top of his lungs. "MOM!!!!!!!!!!!!!!!!!!
His mouth becomes so large that it covers half his face.
I've never seen my son the way he is right now.
I've never heard "Mom" like I am hearing it now.
He's absolutely terrified.

This is the moment.
The moment I realize our reality has changed.
Life as we know it will never be the same again.

I slowly walk up the stairs to Axel.
It's hard to climb the stairs as the steps are full of rubble, shards of glass, parts of sinks and debris.
Axel has rushed down the stairs.
We meet on the second floor.

We look at each other and then he gently puts his arm around my waist.

"Mom, you're so injured." His voice is quiet, soft and worried.

I gently put my arm around him, holding the plastic cover in a firm grip with my other hand.

"Axel, where's Anton?" My voice is not as strong as I'd wished it to be.

"My big brother is dead! My big brother has drowned!" He screams out loud, his voice is filled with fear. Tears flow down his pale cheeks and his little body begins to shake. He's in shock.

I understand Anton is not here.

The insight makes my body freeze.

It hits me like a fist punch in my stomach and one straight into my heart. The inner belief and strength that I had built up, is replaced by an ice-cold sensation of fear.

The thoughts spin around and around in my mind.

What does Axel know that I don´t? What is he feeling? What has he seen?

I do everything in my power to sound wise and confident.

"Axel, I'm sure Anton has not drowned." My voice is far from convincing.

I don't ask him about Per, it is obvious that he is not here either.

A young English couple walks towards us. The man tells me that he was by Axel´s side when the wave hit, with his arm around his shoulders.

I look into the man's eyes. He looks so relieved when he realizes that Axel at least has one family member alive.

It must have been a nightmare to stand next a small child who thinks the whole family has died.

Axel does not speak English, he is only in second grade, so they have not been able to talk to each other.

A couple of days later, Axel shares with me, that he thought he would never return to Sweden again. How would people understand that he lives in Sweden, as no one understands Swedish, the only language he speaks?

He's got friendly warm eyes, the English man. I thank him for what he did. It sounds and seems so trivial when I say it.

How do you show your gratitude to a person that was your child's only support during the worst moment in his life? During a time, that for Axel, was an eternity.

We make our way up to the fourth and a half floor, as high as you can get in our building. Axel is next to me, we are side by side, his hand in mine.
On this floor there is only one room, and someone has slammed down the door. We enter the beautiful room overlooking the bay.
It's terrifying to look out over the ocean but that's exactly what we all want to do. We want to make sure we know what's going on because it's not over yet, we all have that feeling even if we still don't understand what just happened.
The ocean might rise again, without any warning.
There is a large King-size bed in the room, it is unmade. I replace the filthy plastic I have had wrapped around my body with a sheet from the bed.
We are ten-twelve persons in the room, many of them Thai people. Four people speaks French, they are all praying to Allah. On the floor below us, twenty people have gathered. There's only one child, that's Axel.

I try to sit down on the bed, but my body hurts too much. So, I try to lay down, but my back is so tense that I can't.
Axel is right next to me. Like he is glued to my body.
I look at him.

My beloved son, you should not have to be this scared. You should not have to look at me with so much worry and fear in your eyes. I would like to tuck you inside my heart and carry you there until we are safe, protect you from everything you see and feel, hear and experience at this moment. Protect you from all the dreadful thoughts that run through your little head...

"Mom, I need to throw up," he says, "I'm so scared I have to throw up."

"It's okay to throw up on the floor if you need to," I had realized that nothing is normal anymore. It is okay to walk into other people's rooms, take their sheets, drink Coca Cola out of their minibar, vomit on their floor.
That also means that we are far away from anything and everything known as normal.
So, what could be the next step from here? What else will be allowed when all unwritten and written rules no longer apply? When life and death are so present?
What if we need to make choices – is it going to be my life or your life?

It feels like water's dripping from my left eye. I take a piece of the sheet that I have wrapped around me to wipe it off.
As I look at it, I see no water, it's blood.
I decide to avoid all the mirrors in the room. I don't want to lose focus; I need to keep my attention on what's happening around me and Axel.

Suddenly everyone starts screaming hysterically, all the languages are mixed. French, Thai, English. The noise cuts like sharp knives in my ears. Panic fills the air, it's difficult to breathe.
I look into the eyes of grown men and what I see is pure fear and agony.
The situation is insane.
I look out through the panoramic window and see the ocean level rising. Up, up!
It does not look like a wave coming at us, rather like someone put a giant hose in the ocean and just fills it up with masses of water. The level is rising fast. No one knows at what level it'll stop. If we are up high enough or not.
The water is grayish black. Rooftops, rubble and debris are thrown around by the wild currents and I think: "What if there are dead people in the water. What if someone died?"
A man starts trying to knock down the ceiling in our room. As soon as he's made a hole in the roof, they help two women and Axel to get up there, so that they are as high up as possible.

I try to sit on the bed, beneath the hole in the roof so that I can keep on talking to Axel, to keep him calm. To let him know that I am still here.

"Is everything OK, Axel? I'm sitting right here. I'm here on the bed. I'm not going anywhere."

As I talk to him, I try to figure out what to do, but I can't think of anything. The concern about where Per and Anton are, I push that away, try to convince myself time and time again that everything is fine, that they are safe. They MUST be safe. I don't let any other thoughts or feelings in because then I would lose my control completely.

After a few minutes, the level of the ocean begins to sink. Just as unexpectedly as it rose. It's all so unreal.

From now on, worry and terror will not leave me alone for a second. The ocean has shown us that it is not over, that at any time without warning, this can happen again. At any moment the water of death could hit. Dangerous, deadly, and impossible for us to fight. Nature's got the power and we have absolutely nothing to oppose.

After a while, I don't know for how long, two men help Axel and the two women down from the roof. We hug each other.

"Mom, they made me smell something strong before I climbed up through the hole." I have no idea what it might have been, but he doesn't seem to be dizzy or affected by it.

"Come, sit here with me." I put my arm around him and pull my fingers through his hair. My mind is spinning, I can't figure out what to do. What's the next step?

After a while, Axel walks out onto the open space outside the room.

I suddenly hear Pers voice. He screams as loud as he can.

"Axel, where's Mom??"

"She's here!" Axel yells back.

My heart is pounding so hard I can feel it in all parts of my body.

I try to get up from the bed as fast as possible. But it's hard. My body is stiff and doesn't want to obey me.

"Where is Anton???" I scream as loud as I can to make sure Per hears me.
"He's with me, on the roof of the main building of the hotel."
My chest and throat fill up with tears and emotions.
I have been terrified due to the uncertainty about Anton.
Thoughts and feelings, I refused to take in , managed to prevent me from panicking, but now they are flowing freely inside of me...
Thank God...
Anton is alive...
Anton is alive...
Thank God...
A warm calming feeling fills my chest, replacing my own voice trying to convince me of something I do not know.
Anton is alive.
I could not have fooled myself for much longer. Panic was lurking behind the corner.
"I need to return to Anton; we'll have to find each other later."
Per is gone again.
I didn't manage to get up from the bed, so I didn't see him but now I know, everyone is still alive.
All four of us have made it so far.

Axel brings me a pair of panties from our room.
It takes some time to put them on. I am struggling to get my body to obey.
I get stiffer and stiffer with every hour passing.
We are lying on the bed, Axel and I. Holding each other's hand, looking at each other.
We don't talk much.
The Frenchmen are talking to a Thai man. I think he works at the hotel; I recognize the shirt. He's got a walkie-talkie in his hand, from which we all can hear people constantly screaming in fear. I try to get some information from him, but he doesn't speak very good English.
What is going on? What is happening? What do they say to each other in Thai?
Is there a new wave coming?
How high is it?

The French men are busy making an escape plan. I understand French. Their plan is to go to the jungle, who is going with them?

One Frenchman, tall and heavily built, has found a life jacket for children that he managed to pull over his much too large body. It looks so strange. Desperate and alarming.

The man with the walkie-talkie wants to join them.

"You will stay here with us, right?" I make sure he understands exactly what I am trying to tell him. You do not leave a child and a wounded mother by themselves. You just don't do that.

"We can't take her and the child with us." I hear them whispering in French.

I understand. They are referring to my injuries.

I don't want to escape to the jungle with them.

All I want is to find and gather my family.

That's the only thing that matters right now.

People start to leave. After a while it's just me, Axel and three men left on this floor.

I make a decision.

We are going to leave.

We are going to find Per and Anton.

We start to walk down the aisle, down the stairs.

I feel lightheaded as if I'm about to faint. I'm about to throw up, the world is spinning around me and there is a buzzing sound in my ears.

We run into some Thai men. They notice that I don't feel too well. A mattress is pulled out from a room and they try to make me lie down on it so that they can carry me down the stairs.

But I don't want to lie down. Absolutely not. I don't want to lose control and be dependent on other people. I want to walk by myself.

Two Thai men grab my arms in a firm grip to support me and we start walking down the stairs. Another Thai man carries Axel on his back.

The stairs are full of broken glass and debris and we are barefoot. As I look down to try to avoid the sharpest shards, I see my own feet. I haven't looked at them before. I see sharp cuts and bleeding, but I don't feel any pain. This does not affect me or the way I look at my ability to move in any way. I decide not to let my injuries and wounds stop me.

As soon as we reach ground floor, we quickly begin to move along the path towards the main building.

Fear hits me as soon as my feet touch the ground, the feeling invades my body and mind. I panic out of pure fear.

I realize that if another wave would hit the island now, we are doomed. There is no time for us to get up high enough, to be safe.

The panic gets worse and worse with every little step I take. I try to run, but I feel as if the Thai men, all meaning well, are stopping me rather than helping me.

I start screaming, I can't help it. I can't stop it.

"Let me go! I want to walk by myself! The water might come! The water might come!!" I scream so loud that my voice is cracking up.

In the middle of the chaos, I look up and see Per and Anton in front of me.

The gratitude over them, that they are alive, my love for them... my emotions drown in my panic.

For hours I have dreamed about hugging Anton, smelling his scent, seeing with my own eyes that he is alive. That he made it.

But now, when he is in front of me, I am completely unable to show him that. Unable to do what a mother is supposed to do, what I would have done.

Should have done.

Instead of hugging him, I rush with two Thai men by my side, their hands still in a tight grip around my arms. I don't even know where I am going anymore, the only thing I know is that I need to go up, up, up!

My reaction is completely bizarre.

I will never forgive myself for not staying with Anton when we met...

That I didn't hug him.

My son.
My child.
My first panic attack.
The only thing on my mind is to get to the main building,
that's all I'm thinking about.
So, I run for it.
The Thai man with Axel on the back is running to keep my
pace.

We reach an open space in the main building where a
gathering place has been made for the injured.
They put me down on a blue plastic mattress from the sun
loungers by the pool. When I lay there, I let my eyes slowly
sweep over my family, absorb them; Per, Anton and Axel.
I have calmed down; I take some deep breaths to get oxygen
into both my brain and my lungs. I don't speak. I just look at
my two children.
They are alive. They are still here.
I investigate every inch of their bodies and faces with my eyes.
I don't find any injuries.
I wonder what Anton's been through. Where did he go?
What did they see, hear and think?
How on earth did they survive?
An American guy with a big black eye kneels by my side. From
now on I think every person approaching me is a doctor. He
asks me some questions; I don't know what I answer.
Per and the man start examining my body, looking through
every inch, pouring Iodine on all my injuries. I guess it stings,
but it doesn't matter right now.
I don't feel any pain.

There's a lot of people gathered here. Probably about a
hundred people. For some reason, they move me up half a
floor. The woman lying next to me has a damaged pelvis. I see
how she disappears into unconsciousness over and over again.
The man sitting by her side looks at me. His eyes are filled
with fear, he is so concerned and worried about his girlfriend.
I feel so bad for him, for her.

We are isolated on this island. How are the seriously injured going to stay alive until we get help? It is obvious to all of us that we are far away from a hospital.

There is a white wooden table right next to me, with piles of towels and other things needed to take care of the injured. A heavily built older man comes walking towards the table. I see him approaching and think that he is probably going to fetch something from the table. Instead he sits down on it.

As I have my head under the table, I see how the table give way due to the man's weight and I scream out loud, in panic: "No, no, no!!"

In this dangerous unreal world, that I exist in right now, I believe that the table and the man will fall on top of me. My scream is bursting with panic and fear, filling the entire floor. All activity stops.

The only person that understands why I'm screaming is the man with the pelvic-injured girlfriend. He calls out to the older man to move away from the table. The man looks at me as if I am a crazy person and walks away.

I understand my behavior is strange, but I don't have it in me right now to be ashamed.

It has now been a couple of hours since the first wave hit. We can hear helicopters in the air and we got the information that they are throwing down medicine and bandages.

Evacuation of the most severely injured has probably begun.

"Marie, I'm going to go up to our room and get my phone so we can call home." Per looks at me.

"No, you can't leave us, I will not let you go down on the ground!"

The very thought of him leaving us is terrifying.

"It will only take a few minutes; I will check carefully both ways to see that it is all clear. That there's not a new wave coming. I swear to God!"

With those words, he is off.

I can see in my children's faces that it does not feel good for them to be alone with me, being injured and strange.

Per stands for safety and security and he knows that, so he hurries back to us.

"You see, it didn't take long? But now I remember why we left my phone in the room today. I don't have any battery left. Shit! We can only make one phone call. So, who do we call?"
I'm thinking for a while. Hmm... It must be someone that we know will pick up and answer right away. Someone who can make sure everyone is contacted in our family. It's 8.15am in Sweden. I am sure everyone's still asleep and no one's worried yet. No one has heard the news.
"Let's call Sofie," I say. Sofie is a friend of the family. She knows everyone and will be structured enough to make sure everyone gets the information.
"Do you want to make the call?" Per hands me the cellphone.

I feel quite calm and collected when I dial her number. I haven't decided exactly what to say to her, the only thing in my mind is to start talking as soon as she answers so that I can share as much information as possible before the phone shuts down.
"Sofie..." Her voice is sleepy, I woke her up.
Hearing her familiar voice, in bed in the safety of Sweden is just too much. The chaos around us becomes even more tangible in contrast with her voice. I'm starting to cry desperately; I can hardly speak.
"You have to call everyone, Sofie." I take some deep breaths and try to talk slowly. The kids look at me with big, scared eyes.
"Has something happened?"
"There has been an earthquake, and lots of water. Don't forget to call Per's parents. We'll call you back later. We are all alive."
I cry nonstop and I talk fast. I repeat the same information over and over again.
We hang up after a few minutes and I understand that Sofie is sitting in her bed in Sweden, understanding absolutely nothing.
Per and I look at each other and we think the same thing. We are alive right now, but this is not over yet, we know that, and it is a terrible awareness and feeling.

I am convinced that what we have been through, you can only survive once. If we were to be caught in one more wave, we're not going to make it.

I hope the children don't feel the same way, but I'm afraid that's exactly what they both think.

They have put a bandage over the hole in my hip. The bandage is not taped to my skin, it's loose, kept in place only by my panties. To make sure it's still there, that I haven't lost it, my hand returns to the hip over and over again. I get a feeling of safety every time I feel the bandage.

I have a cut about 2.5 inches long and 1 inch deep into my right knee. Per has tied a cloth napkin from the restaurant around that knee. It slides down as soon as I move and that annoys me.

What I don't see, doesn't exist – that became my survival mantra in the hotel room when I realized there was blood dripping into my eye and that I will hold onto as long as I am stuck on this island.

I feel okay with my injuries. They don't scare me.

But I don't want to see them.

There are rumors of new waves all the time.

"The next wave will hit at 11am and it will be 50 feet high."

Time passes slowly. Everybody's focusing on the sound of the ocean.

The clock is ticking... tic toc, tic toc, tic toc

10.50...

10.55...

Hearts are beating hard.

We are all waiting for the wave to hit us.

Our pulse is rushing. Fear has us all in a firm grip.

Nobody talks.

Everyone's waiting.

It's 11am sharp.

No wave...

But no one dares to relax. Since when does nature care about the clock?

A young woman from the reception collects information from guests. Name, nationality, room number.

She informs Per that the injured should remain here, at the hotel, for evacuation but those who can walk should go up to the heights of the jungle.

We are too far away from the part of the island where the jungle is accessible, where there are roads, we are closer to the part of the jungle where humans are not supposed to walk.

"There's a wave hitting us at 2pm and it's 10 feet high," she informs us before she moves on. The information is spreading like wildfire.

"Per! I want to go to the jungle! NOW! I'm exhausted of being terrified!"

"But you can't walk that far, Marie. Don't you understand that? You are badly hurt. We have to stay here so you can go with a helicopter to a hospital!" He speaks to me with a serious voice, trying to make me understand the situation.

"No, I don't want to stay here, and I can walk!" I sound like a rebellious five-year-old. I'm very determined.

From now on, it's obvious that we have different priorities. For me, the first and only priority is for the family to stay together. To be close to our children.

Nothing else matters to me.

For Per, who has got a more realistic perspective, my injuries and need for medical attention are priority No. 1.

I refuse to listen to him.

The jungle

I don't want to stay here.
I have made up my mind.
We are going to the jungle.
After a while Per gives in. He realizes that there is no point in trying to change my mind.
With his help, I manage to get up from the plastic mattress I've been lying on. There's not a lot of people left here. I have no idea where they have gone.
We start to walk down the stairs. I'm unable to move fast.
I don't complain, I don't say a word. It doesn't hurt; I just have a hard time to move my body.
There is glass everywhere. Someone gives me a pair of soft morning slippers.
Per runs off to our room to get some tracksuits and shoes for Anton and Axel.
As soon as we put our feet on the ground, two things happen.
The first is the fear that hits us.
The fear of being on the ground again is overwhelming. If a new wave should hit the island while we are on our way to the jungle, we will die. No doubt about that. There's no chance of survival.
We are a small group of people walking together across the devastated land towards the height of the jungle. I feel that they are moving too slowly, I hear myself repeating out loud, that we need to hurry up! Move faster, to get to a safer place.
The second thing that happens is the realization of how the island has been affected by the tsunami – there used to be houses, bungalows, and palm trees where we are walking. It's all gone now.
The hospital next to our hotel has vanished.
Just like that.
Gone.
We walk across the concrete ground where it used to be four hours ago. The sight is unbearable.

The path is not straight. We walk between piles of rubble and over walls that were previously part of houses. My head moves from side to side, right, left, right, left. There is a blue lagoon on each side of us. The wave can hit us any time, from any direction, so I need to constantly see the bays, see the ocean.
I don't feel any of my injuries, I could have, would have run if the environment would let me.
We walk by a pile of what would have been a bungalow, as we pass it, there is a sudden crashing noise as part of the broken roof falls. The unexpected sound makes us all jump high.
As I look over towards the right bay, I see a young dead Thai woman.
She lies on her back with her arms along her sides.
Her clothes are green, she has long dark beautiful hair.
It's surreal, I can't believe it's real.
That what I see, is what exists.

We finally reach the jungle and see that the last row of bungalows in the island has made it. The wave did not reach this part. My conclusion is that as soon as we reach the jungle, we are safe.
We start walking. It's steep. There is no path, we walk through branches, over roots, surrounded by lianas.
It's difficult to move ahead.
We are about fifty persons on our way to safety higher up in the jungle. Mostly Thai people, but I also hear some Swedish far away.
At the border of the steep jungle, someone has put down a large mattress to be used for the injured, for those who can't walk into the jungle. I feel so sorry for them.
I would never want to stay down there!
Per stops to help a man who is severely injured, they put him down carefully on the mattress.

As it is steep, we need to pull ourselves up using the lianas hanging from the trees. Some of them are weak so we test them to know if they will hold us before we rely on them. That takes a lot of time but that's okay, because with every step we manage to take, we get almost three feet higher up from the ground level, that's how steep it is. It could not have been better; I think to myself.

Up, up up – that's all I want.

The napkin around my injured knee keeps slipping down.

A man next to me pulls it back up, he ties it really tight so that it stays in place.

We have not seen Per for a while now and I can see how that concerns Anton and Axel. But I keep on climbing uphill with them regardless.

I know Per will catch up with us.

I'm starting to feel safe.

I believe we are at least sixty-five feet above sea level by now. Some people decided to camp further down the hill, but I kept going upwards. I want good margins.

When we have reached about 150 feet above ground level, we set camp. I cannot walk any further. I need to get my head down and feet up preventing me from fainting.

Some Thai women, men and children are also here. Some of them must have been here for a while, there are some bonfires burning around us.

I understand this is a place with snakes. I am concerned that we don't have Anton's medication. What if something bites him and he gets an allergic reaction here in the jungle.

I decide to try blocking those thoughts as I cannot do anything about it.

We sit on the right side of the "path".

The ground is hard, rocky, there're roots everywhere.

My body aces when I try to lay down.

Anton and Axel are close to me, so I try to hide my pain not to worry them.

I am beyond grateful when I suddenly see Per coming towards us. He's got a bedsheet wrapped around his neck.

"Try to stand up Marie. I will put the sheet under you, so that you don't get dirt into your wounds. Can you do that? If you put your arm around my neck, I'll lift you up."

"I can't stand up right now, I'm about to faint. See if you can sit in front of me with your back towards me so that I can put my legs on your shoulders? I really need to raise them up."

"Okay. And you need to drink something. It's really important that you don't get dehydrated, Marie" He bends down over the backpack and picks up a Swedish snuff-box, with moist powdered tobacco. "Do you want some?"

Yes, I do. I'd love some.

"When and how did you get it?"

"I picked it up when I went back to our room before we left."

It takes a lot of effort, but after a while I am able to put my legs on his shoulders. My nausea and dizziness slowly fade away and my head begins to feel clearer.

It's quiet around us. The only thing we hear is the snapping sounds from the bonfire and whispering voices.

This is so good! We are at such a good place right now. Axel is lying next to me; I caress his back, trying to share a feeling of safety, from me to him. He seems so small in the middle of all this chaos.

I want to protect him and Anton from the horrible things around us.

I run my fingers through his curls, like I always do.

Trying to assure a feeling that everything's fine, that we have each other and that's the only thing that matters.

If God should descend from heaven right now, and ask me for a favor, there is nothing I would not have done for him.

Everything becomes so clear to me, up here in the jungle.
Who I am.
What I want.
How I want to live my life.
My priorities.
My gratitude.

I promise from now on I will be a better person, I will not stress as much as I have done, I will not worry so much about small things, I will live my life in a different way – I am going to value life more than I have ever done.

From now on, gratitude of being alive will be my guiding star and I will always follow my heart.

I'm going to quit my job and get a new one when I get home. No job in the world is worth the time I have spent away from my children. That way of living life stops here and now. Never again.

And from now on, I will choose the people I have around me, never again will I invite people to dinner that I don't really, really like. And those that are close to me, I will make them my priority.

I look around. We are surrounded by kind eyes, warmth, and a strong sense of community. We share the same fears, the same chance and the same risk. There is no mine or yours here in the jungle.

Water bottles are shared. A bag of buns is sent around. A young man hands Anton a thick comic book in Thai. That comes in handy as toilet paper later that night.

After a while Per helps me to get up from the ground. He puts the sheet under me, and I lie down again. I feel like a heavy rock. As soon as I stand up, I am about to faint. I am sweating all over the place, and my hearing disappears.

After about three hours we move a little bit further down, I do not really know why. Maybe because there is more space and more people. We make sure to be close to one of the bonfires to keep the mosquitoes and snakes away.

Per starts to unpack the backpack he brought with him from our room. Anton and Axel put on their tracksuits. Per helps me to put on my Thai pants.

As I have lost the morning slippers that protected my wounded feet from insects and dirt, Per puts plastic bags around them instead.

A middle-aged woman from South Africa is sitting next to me.
She's all alone, her entire family including her grandchildren
has disappeared. They are gone.
She is just wearing a swimsuit, so we give her some of our
clothes to keep her warm.
She is in shock. Her body is shaking. She's sad and lonely,
we're doing everything we can to just be there, with her.

The darkness settles over the jungle, from daylight to dark
night in thirty minutes. Anton and Axel slumber next to me.
Per sits in front of me, still with my feet on his shoulders.
I caress my children, over and over again, with so much
gratitude. It feels like I gave birth to them once again.
That's how powerful my emotions are.
I will later on describe the hours in the jungle as the happiest
hours of my life and I will remember the feeling as long as I
shall live. And then some more. The contrast between the
trauma we survived and the gratitude of everyone in the family
being alive, black and white, life and death.
Our plan from the start is for us to spend the night high up in
the jungle. And that's exactly what I want.
I even fantasize about never going down to the ground level
again. If we go even higher up there might be space for a
helicopter to fetch us? I'm sure they could wire something
down and lift us up. That kind of thoughts gives me peace of
mind.
Never touch the ground again, that's exactly what I want.

It's a full moon.
A huge ball of silver shines down on us, through the leaves,
throwing dusts of silver on every person around us.
It's beautiful.
The only thing that concerns me right now is the sound of the
ocean. I look down at the valley to try to keep track of the
water level. All around us, people are sending text messages.
The light from the mobiles lights up the dark.
Per and I are whispering to each other about all the friends
that also are here in Thailand on vacation right now.
We wonder how everyone is doing.

The rumors are intense and limitless: Koh Lanta is underwater. Phuket is completely swept away, everyone died. The airport is below sea level... It goes on and on.

It is now nine o'clock in the evening and according to the latest information, this is the time when the next wave will hit Phi Phi Island. The wave is estimated to be sixty-five feet high when it strikes.
I focus my hearing so that I only hear the ocean and the sound of the waves. Didn't this wave sound a little louder than the previous one?
As I look down between the trees, suddenly I see in the moonlight that the sea level is higher. I can see through the leaves on the trees, people floating around. I see their backs in the moonlight. Ten-fifteen dead bodies floating around. My heart starts pounding.
"Per, look, look what happened... lots of people... drowned, the sea is high..."
I do my best to whisper even though I am so scared that my whole being is screaming.
He looks down, try to see what I just witnessed.
I'm shaking.
I must be quiet; I don't want to scare the children.
Before Per says anything, I see.
I see that it is the moonlight's reflections that fooled me.
It's not the backs of dead people, it's the moon that shines on the leaves in the trees.
My heart calms down, I move closer to Per, feeling so tiny and scared.
I don't wear a watch; time seems to pass by very slowly. Every now and then one or two people leave the heights of the jungle. I don't know where they are going.
Everybody is asking each other the obvious question: "Have you heard anything? Do you know anything?"

At midnight, an American woman is shouting from below: "There's a boat coming in that will take 200 people. A man called Mario has found a safe way to get to the pier, he has a torch in his hand. Follow him."

I shake my head. "I don't want to go down, Per. I want to stay here and then maybe we can go down tomorrow."

"But if there is a boat, of course we're going to take it Marie. You need to go to the hospital. They wouldn't tell us to go down if it wasn't safe. I promise."

I don't believe for a second that anyone knows the exact time for the next wave and I really don't want to leave the height of the jungle.

To convince myself that we are safe, I think out loud: "We felt the earthquake in the morning, right? I felt my bed shaking?" Per nods. "The wave hit after about two hours. We have laid down on the ground here in the jungle for many hours by now. If there had been another earthquake, we would have felt it. But we haven't noticed any shaking and even if we did, it would take two hours for the wave to arrive."

I try to be logical and rational, but my heart does not trust my head.

More and more people start passing us as they walk down, finally we decide to leave the jungle for the boat.

"Anton and Axel..." I softly touch them as they sleep next to me. It feels so wrong to wake them up." We are leaving the jungle. A man with a torch will take us to a boat."

I can see how they instantly go back to the state they were in on the way to the jungle. How fear and nervousness come into their eyes and it hurts me so much that I expose them to this. Will this nightmare never end??

They quietly take our hands, do not protest as we leave the safety of the jungle.

My mind is screaming inside my head "NO, I DO NOT WANT TO GO DOWN!! I want us to stay here!!"

Leaving the jungle

It is not easy to walk down the steep ground with thick roots everywhere and my feet in slippery plastic bags.
Per walks in front of me so that I can have my hands on his back.
I still don't feel any pain from my injuries, the only thing on my mind is that I need to be ready to fight for our lives.
Anything can happen, I need to be ready.
Fully focused on where the children are, where the ocean is, how the ocean sounds.
I'm preparing for full readiness mentally...
When we get down, we spot Mario, the man who's going to take us to the boat.
The full moon light is not enough. We need help from Mario to light up where we walk.
The ground is covered in parts of walls, glass, nails, air condition machines, broken boats, boards... There are large holes in the ground.
We move slowly like a swirling snake, down by the beach. The same beach where we were standing when the wave took us.
I have to fight my mind, which is screaming at me:
"Are you completely insane? HOW CAN YOU PUT YOUR CHILDREN THROUGH THIS? HOW ON EARTH CAN YOU LEAVE THE SAFETY OF THE JUNGLE AND GO DOWN TO THE GROUND LEVEL AGAIN?"
As soon as we get a little separated, the children get worried, even though we can see each other.
Once down by the shore, we walk along the sea, in some places we must go out into the ocean to get past all the rubble that lies in large piles.
I have lost the plastic bags and I can see my bare wounded feet in the moonlight.
Are they really mine?
How strange they look.

Someone has wrapped a bandage around one of my feet, it has loosened and the flap from the bandage floats around on the surface of the sea as I walk.

I look out over the horizon.

I hate the sound of the waves slowly hitting the beach.

We are approaching our hotel. A white concrete skeleton covered in the moon's silver glow, deserted and abandoned. Devastated but still the only building that's left here.

When we reach the pool area in front of the hotel, we need to climb a wall. I move and feel like I weigh several tons. Per pulls me up and a man pushes me from behind. So here I am again. The same spot as this morning, by the pool. I shiver all over my body.

The kids are a bit ahead of us. "Stay where you are, don't go any further! Wait for us."

It is quiet, except for the frightening sounds from the ocean. A scary cold silence. We walk around the hotel towards what used to be the hotel's tennis court but now serves as the landing platform for helicopters.

I look around me. I don't know exactly what was here before, just that every square meter of the island was covered by something and now everything is swept away.

I see across the island, from bay to bay.

There are two piers, one old and one new. First, we are told to go to the old one because the new pier is not safe after the Tsunami hit. We walk around to the front of our hotel and the devastation is even larger on this side. Probably because the wave hit first and hardest on our side, so a lot of the debris was flushed over here from the other side. It is very difficult to walk here.

Anton is doing everything he can to make sure a man who has a flashlight stays close to me so I can see where I put my feet. He seems so grown up in the middle of all the chaos, eleven years old he takes command and I follow him.

I let my eyes rest on him for a while.

My heart fills with love.

I'm so proud of him.

He's going to be such an extraordinary man when he grows up! Strong, soft, confident, and full of empathy.
The moon shines on his beautiful curls as he walks in front of me.

Dear God, I love him so much..
Thank you for choosing me as his mom.
For letting me live my life with him!
For letting me keep him...

Once we get closer to the old pier, we just stand there, all of us desperately looking for the boat that are supposed to get us from here, to safety.
But there's no boat in sight.
Out in the bay there is a white house with a green roof floating around. We can see boat lanterns shining in the dark, but those boats are far away from our island.
"We'll have to go to the new pier; the boat can't get in here. There's too much debris floating around in the bay." The American woman who brought us down from the jungle leads us away. What worries me is that there is no boat nearby, so what is she talking about? No one asks that question even though everyone wonders.
Every time we pass by our hotel, I get shivers all along the spine, it looks like a ghost castle, abandoned, huge and dark. We go through the reception area, it's the only path that is possible to use on this side of the island, I look into the hotel – it's pitch-black.

When we are getting close to the pier, we are stepping onto high unstable piles of sticks, swaying dangerously wherever we put our feet. At any moment, everything could collapse.
What if someone is under all this rubble?
I shudder and balance gently on a long board, it sways alarmingly with every step I take.
Nails point straight out of the debris, I step on one, my foot gets stuck.
It doesn't hurt, I don't feel anything, I just pull out the nail from my foot, and continue to walk.

We arrive at the other pier, located at the beginning of the village. All the buildings by the main street have collapsed under the weight and power of the two waves that hit from both sides and met here in the middle of the island. The sight is unreal and horrible.

As I look out over the pier, the warning bells I heard earlier are ringing in my ears "The pier is unsafe, the water has undermined the entire pier."

We are receiving new information. "Go back again, the same way you came. The boat cannot come in here either. Be careful not to rush. Look where you put your feet!"

After balancing the same route back, people gather in an open space between the two bays. We are around fifty persons, in different ages and different countries.

I spot the older South American woman from the jungle. She is still wearing Anton's pink Thai pants around her shoulders.

We give each other a hug, in silence but so much is communicated between us. She looks lonely and I have my family by my side.

The injustice of how the disaster struck becomes so clear.

We sit down on a pile of debris and let our eyes take in the surrounding.

The full moon illuminates the devastation around us. There's a lunar reflection out in the bay, on the debris floating around.

I don't know for how long we sit here. Maybe fifteen minutes. My wounded feet are still bleeding. A woman comes up to me. She doesn't say anything, just hands me a pair of white socks. I thank her with a soft smile and Per puts them on for me.

It's so quiet on the island.

Those who talk do so with low-key voices, as out of respect to all those who are no longer heard at all.

I realize there will be no boat.

Someone says: "We' are stuck here for the night."

I understand, but I don't want to accept it. But what choice do we have? None of what happened today was a choice. Neither did we have the power or control over it.

I can no longer see the end of this chaos; it feels like it will continue forever.

We walk back to our hotel, the haunted house, and there is a burst of discomfort in my body as I begin to enter the darkness. I know I am walking on sharp pieces of glass, but I don't feel it. I send gratitude to the woman who gave me the socks that protects my feet a little.

Slowly we start climbing the stairs at the hotel, one floor at a time. On the top floor there is an open space, like a large loft aisle with a circular opening like an atrium courtyard. The fence is three feet high, and you can see between the ribs out to the bay where the boat will arrive and eventually save us. We all want to be able to see the ocean and the boat when it appears.

Some men start kicking in the doors to the rooms so that we can get drinks and chocolates and other things that may be needed. Mattresses are pulled out onto the open space as well as sheets and pillows.

I find a chair along the corridor on the left.

Climbing the stairs has left me with a feeling of fainting. I have no strength left.

A French family is next to me, their son has a flashlight in his hand, and he points the light towards me. I have lost the bandage around my wounded knee, leaving the cut into my flesh open and visible.

I see that my flesh has started to change color from red to beige.

It looks strange. Is it really supposed to look like that?

The French mother helps me up from the chair and leads me away towards their room.

Anton and Axel are close to me.

We lie down on their double bed while the family walks around in the torch light and pack their things. They talk about not forgetting their traveler's checks.

Anton and Axel fall asleep by my side, both exhausted.

Per comes into the room. "We have found food down in the restaurant, rice and stuff and lots of water. We can survive here for quite a while."

I see his silhouette in the dark. "Per, we are not going to have to eat here, are we? I mean, it won't be that long until they come for us, right?"

"I have no idea when they will, honestly. You heard what they said, there is too much debris in the water so the boats can't get in here. But don't worry, it's going to be fine, we are okay up here."

I begin to cry, tears run down my cheeks and my body starts shaking. "I want to get out of here. I don't want to be here anymore."

I try to cry as quietly as I can so I don't wake the children, but I can't stop the tears anymore. Now that the kids are asleep, I don't have to pretend to be brave and strong.

Per sits down by the bed and puts his hand on my cheek.

"I'm so scared, Per, so terribly scared. What if there is another wave coming?"

"If there's another wave, it's not as high as the others, and we're safe up here, I promise."

I don't trust him. How could he possibly know how safe we are on the fourth floor? I don't rely on logic or guesswork right now. It feels like nature has rebelled against humanity.

What if this is a punishment for how we treat mother nature? The French family has gone to bed in different places in the room and I hear their deep breathing. I feel like I'm bothering them with my sobbing, and I want to talk more to Per, sleeping is the last thing I want to do right now.

We go out from the room, leaving the door open so that I can keep an eye on the kids.

Per gets a large double mattress from a room and we lie down on it. I'm starting to relax a little. We lie there in the moonlight completely silent, holding hands.

Per, who has been in the military, always brings an emergency kit when we travel. We've always made a little fun of him around the kit that is filled with tee three oil, small candles, string, a Swiss knife, matches and some other things that might be good to have but now it's clear to us all why the bag is important. His candles are arranged around the loft aisle, spreading a warm light in the dark night.

I look around, some people are sitting in groups talking quietly while their eyes rest on the ocean.

After an hour we hear voices from the stairs, some people are on their way up to us. It turns out to be an American and an English doctor who, together with a nurse, walks around the island to find injured persons.
"Are there any casualties here?"
"Yes, my wife. She is right here next to me." Per says.
"Where is she hurt?"
"She's got cuts everywhere, the biggest are in her knee and her right hip."
"Has she received any help? Someone who washed the wounds?" The two doctors examine my injuries, they pull down my panties and lift the bandage from my hip. They ask for better light so that they can see properly.
I start to breath heavily; it hurts when they touch me.
"You need to get out of here as soon as possible. There will be a boat at three o'clock tonight and you need to embark that boat. It will bring injured people to the hospital in Phuket."
"My family will come with me."
"No, there's only room for casualties."
"Then I'll stay here, I'm not going anywhere without them."
Tears begin to roll down my cheeks.
I see in the older man's eyes that if I go down to the boat, it is going to be fine. I will be able to bring my family.
"We need to clean with iodine again. You have been walking around with open wounds in the heat for many hours. It's going to hurt, are you ready?"
I nod, hug Per's hand tightly and continue with the heavy breathing that I was taught before giving birth.
A Norwegian woman sits by my side, caressing my arm to comfort me. She gives me juice to drink between each wound they disinfect.
When they have cleaned up all major wounds with iodine, one doctor says to the other: "We need to stitch her up."
"We have only thread; we didn't get any needles."

In the meantime, almost everyone around us has disappeared, the information about the boat at 3am must have set them off towards the piers.

Now it's a real struggle for me to get up from the mattress. The only way for it to work is when Per bends down over me and pulls me up onto my feet.

We wake the kids up. "There's a boat coming to pick us up. Take your stuff and let´s hurry." The kids don't want to leave the safety of being asleep, they don't want to wake up to this never-ending nightmare.

It takes a while to walk down the stairs. All flashlights disappeared with the people that already left so we are navigating through the debris in total darkness.

As soon as we reach the ground, we head for the pier, but we don't get far until we meet hysterical people running our way, back to the hotel. The air fills with panic. "There's a new wave coming our way! The wave is coming! Run!"

By now, we are mentally set in emergency mode when it comes to running for our lives. So, we start running. But for the first time I also feel that my fear is mixed up with pure anger. What the hell is this?! What the hell is going on????

I run the best I can, thinking this cannot be true, this cannot happen. When is this hell going to end???

When we get back to the open space on the fourth floor, Per and I look at each other and we decide that enough is enough, we'll have to stay here until tomorrow. The children lie down by my side on a mattress and Per brings out a chair next to us.

Many times during the night the waves suddenly sound a little more than they did before and my heart behaves as it's been doing so many times in this chaos, it beats so hard that I can feel it in my fingertips. It beats so loud that it's the only thing I can hear at times. I'm so afraid of what might happen. Even if the next wave is not as high as the previous ones, there is heavy large debris floating around in the bay, boats and houses. What would happen if the wave is only 10 feet high, but comes at us with full speed throwing a boat at the hotel, what happens then? Couldn't that be what finally makes the remaining walls to fall apart?

"Marie, if there is a new wave coming, take the children to the staircase. It's the safest place." Per whispers not to wake the children.
"But you said there won't be any more waves." I sound like a child.
"I know. But IF I'm wrong, please bring the kids to the staircase. Ok?" I look at the staircase and memorize what I need to do if what's not going to happen, does happen.
Per is in the construction business so he talks a while about building technology. It's nice to talk about something other than natural disasters for a while.

Time passes slowly.
It's quiet around us, everybody is sleeping.
Some snoring and heavy breaths, but other than that, the silence is total.
I try to find a position that doesn't hurt too much, but my body has become stiff and I can't relax.
I feel like I have been in a tough fight.
"Per, I need to go to the toilet. Can you please help me?"
Per bends down over me. I put my arms around his neck and while he rises slowly, I pull my body up. It works, I'm in control.
Once on my feet, the world is spinning. I try to collect myself. Breathe.
Per turns on a flashlight and lights up the corridor where all the hotel doors are knocked down.
We walk into one of the rooms. I have been in this room earlier during the night, but I didn't take the time to look around. I look through the windows towards the bay. I need to see the ocean on that side. As I move through the room, someone's room, it sinks in.
This is someone's room.
There are clothes, bags, hairbrushes ... and children's toys.
My heart stops for a few seconds – I pray everyone is alive.
Maybe the family is safe up in the jungle.
As I look out over the bay, a sadness hit me so heavily that the air I breathe becomes warm.
The ocean lays quiet and dark.

How many lives have been taken today by the ocean?
The thought comes to me without warning, it's like my subconscious mind has blocked those thoughts to protect me.
My tears begin to roll down my cheeks, slowly I turn around and see Per's silhouette in the dark.
I don't know for how long we stand there, in silence.
It's a moment of mourning, a moment for all of those who didn't survive.
Minutes of reflection- What happened today?
When we return, Per helps me lay down on the mattress next to the kids.
The sound of their breathing is so comforting to listen to. My children are here, both, next to me.
I feel their bodies, let my hands wander over them.
 Over and over again.
Time passes, a sense of stillness mixed with fear surrounds us.
Per sits in the chair by my side.
I follow the shadows from the bats flying around us.
"Per, why is it so silent? Why don't all the birds sing? "
Suddenly I'm wide awake and my heart is pounding. It's not supposed to be this quiet!
This is the proof, the proof that the world has gone crazy. Even the birds have escaped.
"The birds don't sing until the sun starts to rise. You'll see."
I don't believe him for a second, he's just trying to calm me down but it's not working.
I just listen, listen to what is not heard.
Time passes so slowly. Every second feels like an hour.
To make sure I don't miss a single sound from nature, I even shut out the sound of my children breathing.
If a new wave is coming, I'm the one that needs to hear the sound.
If the birds start singing again, I'm the one that needs to hear it.
"Marie, please look. The sun begins to rise..."
I lay still, I don't move. I focus on listening...
A couple of minutes passes in silence...
And then suddenly I can hear it... I HEAR THE BIRDS!

A heatwave goes through my body. The world hasn't become insane after all. The universe is still functioning.

That insight gives me energy and determination.

"Per, let's go, let's go down to the pier and just get us out of here."

"If you wake the kids up, I'll gather our things. Do you have something to put on your feet Marie?"

The first mission

Carefully I wake the children up, we don't talk much, we just touch instead. They go from sleeping, to standing up awake in what feels like seconds. As if they've been on high alert even during their sleep.

Young men who apparently slept in some of the rooms quickly disappears down the stairs towards the pier, where the boat hopefully is.

As we walk down the stairs in the morning light, we see the devastation around us. Not a single square meter looks like it did yesterday morning. Everything is ruined. It is completely impossible to understand that less than 24 hours ago this was a fancy hotel and that we sat right here, next to the stairs and had breakfast. Now it´s pure chaos.

Approaching the pier, we look out over the bay. The house that floated around in the water is now gone, I guess it sunk.

My goal is for us to go straight to the pier but a Swedish man, who I naturally think is a doctor, has got hold of Per and asked him to help out with fetching injured people from the village.

I don't understand what suddenly happens, I don´t protest.

I follow Per as he walks toward the tennis court where helicopters are landing. It´s just around the corner but there are big holes in the ground, so we have to walk slowly and carefully.

When we arrive, I am told to sit on one of the mattresses.

In my hand I have a plastic bag that Per handed me, with some money.

My body is stiff. I move like a zombie.

Anton and Axel are close to me.

"Sit down, it´s important that it's never empty or they might stop flying here." The man talks to me in a way that makes me feel stupid.

"If people that are more injured than you come here, you have to move from the mattress. Okay?"

Is this stranger telling me that I should sit in different places to play a role? A piece to be moved around to fill different functions. He doesn't even know where or how hurt I am, it's not visible because I'm wearing my Thai pants and they cover my worst injuries.

I have no energy to spend discussing with him, I just look for Per. He's going to save me from this, get us away from this.

I have heard people around me talk about some helicopters flying to Phuket and others flying to Krabi, so I have no idea where I'm going to end up.

Fear is spreading through my body; I do NOT want to go in a helicopter! I want to go to the pier and take a boat from here with my family.

That's it.

The children are sitting next to me on the mattress, I try to hide my thriving feeling of panic. I can't find Per. I see the ocean on both sides, and it feels terribly wrong and dangerous to sit here. This is the place where it all happened, where everything went wrong and now, I sit here "willingly" again.

Am I out of my mind?

What am I doing?

The kids are unnaturally quiet, I don't recognize my own kids and that increases the feeling of panic.

We walk back to the place where Per put our bag. Anton and Axel sits down on the ground and I have the strangest experience. I take a moment for myself, I just stand still and look up into the sky.

It's bright blue, not a cloud in sight.

The sun is low, it's only 7am in the morning.

I look at the mountains and it's all so beautiful.

Then I lower my eyes and take in the sight of the ruined island.

My brain, my heart cannot grasp the contrasts.

What I see is so completely unreal that it cannot be true.

Per approaches us. "I'm going to carry wounded people from the village. You just stay here, and the helicopter will take you to the hospital, we'll be right behind you, I promise."

"Per. We are going to walk over to the pier and get out of here. Now!!" My voice is hard as steel.

"I will go into the village once, then I´ll come back and take the kids to the pier." I hear he's determined.
Some people suddenly interfere in our discussion. The man who gave me orders on the tennis court is here again. He is also the one that told Per to walk into the village.
He looks at me and says with the coldest of voices: "People are dying here today. At least you still have your children."
I am speechless.
My mind is in chaos.
My whole body, my heart and my soul screams to me; GET OUT OF HERE!! NOW!!
"If I leave in a helicopter and Per is in the village, our children have no parent here. I will not leave them alone." I try to control my voice, but I can't. I sound hysterical.
An American woman promise that she will take care of Anton and Axel until Per returns. Everything is spinning so fast around me. I don't know what's being said, I let myself be led down to the waiting helicopter on the platform after saying goodbye to the children. Their eyes reflect the panic I feel.
This is so wrong!
With the plastic bag in a firm grip and tears running down my cheeks I crawl into the helicopter. The doors are open on both sides. On my left side there is a bench, six persons can sit there. The bench is already full, so I need to sit on my knees on the floor in front of them. I look around. No one looks in my direction, I crawl straight through the helicopter and walk with confident steps back up to my children.
"Mom, didn't you go with the helicopter to the hospital??" In their eyes I see relief, wonder and confusion.
"No, I changed my mind. Have you seen Dad yet? He's going to get us out of here."
We look over at the beach where he disappeared on his way into the village.
How long has it been since he left? How far is it?
I feel an anger growing in my chest. My heart is pounding and beating so hard, so hard. How can he leave us when we need him the most?
Suddenly my "enemies" sees me again.

"Are you still here! You were supposed to be on the helicopter that just left! You need to go back down there again! What kind of mother are you, risking your life like this? If you want to be a good mother, you have to keep yourself alive!!"

A Norwegian woman promise that she will take care of my children until Per comes back.

"You MUST tell Per that he needs to take our children out of here AS SOON AS HE RETURNS!!"

I cannot fight them, I can't find the arguments, the words, the energy, so I give up.

I stumble my way down to the helicopter after once again saying Goodbye to my children.

In my head, their words are spinning around.

About me being a bad mother if I don't leave, my heart screaming the opposite – how could a mother leave her children alone here? Just thinking of her own safety.

What kind of a mother is that?

Isn't a good mother the one who, whatever happens, does everything to stay with her children? To be close to them when they need her the most?

Arriving at the open door of the helicopter, I get on my knees to crawl in on the floor.

The bench is full.

A Swedish father sits next to his teenage son. The son has a bandage around his foot, the father has scratches on his arm. He makes no effort to make room for me on the bench.

I crawl along the aisle; it's crowded and warm and I suddenly become aware of the wound in my knee. It must be wide open when I crawl on the floor. The thought makes my head spin and I feel nauseous.

"Please, be careful. My son's foot is hurt." The father from Stockholm has spoken.

I can't believe it.

What the hell does he think the rest of us are sitting here for? Because it's fun to ride a helicopter?

The only one in this helicopter who doesn't seem to be seriously injured is himself and he's more than happy to take a seat on the bench and let much more injured people crawl on the floor in front of him?

My nausea is amplified just by his presence.

Nobody says anything, no one bothers to answer him.

Suddenly something hits me hard from behind. I turn my head and I see that it's a door used as a stretcher, carrying a very injured man. I feel like I'm in the way, but I have nowhere else to go, I'm already sitting as close to the other opening as I can. The man is in terrible pain.

Right there and then I lose it.

I get a panic attack.

Everything merges, my open wounds, the Swedish father, the injured man, the heat, the blood, my children being all alone.

I gather all the strength I have left in my body, and finally act on what I believe in and really want.

I have made up my mind, once and for all.

If I have to choose between recovering from my injuries but not seeing my children for several days or being with them and pay the price of losing a leg, I don't have to think a second for the answer.

Take my leg and let me be with my children!!

I'm leaving this helicopter and I'm not going back in again!!

What I don't know is that Per is one of the men who brought the injured man, he is one of the men trying to push the stretcher further in to the helicopter, not realizing that I am blocking it. Another Swedish man who we encountered during the night tells Per that it´s me, his wife, sitting there on the floor and maybe Per would like to take the opportunity to say goodbye, before the helicopter takes off.

I finally manage to rise from the floor when Per shows up in front of the helicopter's doorway. Before he has a chance to say anything to me, I scream from the top of my lungs. "I want out!! I need to get out of here!!"

Per tries to stop me from leaving the helicopter by blocking my way. He's got his back towards me and his hands against the helicopter's door frames.

I look at his shaved head below me as I am screaming with a primal voice that comes from the deepest part of me, the part that just want one thing – my children.

It feels like forever.

Like hours.

Nothing happens.

Per doesn't move so I get ready.

I prepare myself to bite his head with my front teeth so that he'll let me go.

Yes, I'm going to use my teeth, it's too late for words.

I will not let anybody stand between me and my children from now on.

I am going to be the strongest person in the world.

From this moment, I am in control, using all the power and strength I can attain to accomplish what I know I must do.

I use every molecule in my body and my soul to gather the energy that will be needed to carry out what lies ahead of me.

Per finally let's go of the doorway and I leave the helicopter.

I walk pass him, down on the ground. I don't look at him, I don't say anything. Instead I walk with military steps, still keeping the plastic bag in a firm grip, towards the children who are relieved to see both Per and me even if everything is crazy and impossible to understand.

Finally, together again!

"Take your things Anton and Axel, we're going to the pier and take a boat out of here."

I feel like I'm a soldier at war.

And I'm going to win this war.

I will NOT be separated from my children one more time.

When we reach the pier, we see several hundred people waiting in a queue. There's a boat at the end of the pier. It that takes up to two hundred people.

I'm determined to walk pass the queue, I don't look in any direction, my eyes are frozen on the boat at the end of the pier.

A young Swedish man in the queue starts screaming at me " What the hell are you doing? We've been here all night. Get in line, damn it!!"

I decide not to listen him.

He doesn't exist in my world.

I'm not entirely sure that Per is behind me, but I don't dare to turn around, I don't want to think that he didn't understand the seriousness. He needs to be right behind me with the children.

There is a Thai man at the end of the pier.
"I need a doctor," I say and pull up my Thai pant to show him my injuries. Without any questions, another Thai man takes my arm in a firm grip and leads me through the queue.
I am the last person onboard the boat.
It´s full now.
There is panic in the air.
I turn around.
Per is a little bit behind with the children. "And my husband and my children."
My voice is sharp as a knife.
It's not a question, it's an order.
There is no discussion, Per and the children are bypassing the queue and boarded the boat.
The first mission is complete.
My head is spinning so fast.
Now it's just my next missions left to achieve.

Phuket hospital

The boat is overloaded.

There are people everywhere.

We walk down the aisle towards the bow of the boat where the life jackets are. Everyone's wearing life jackets, even if most of them are broken and lack buckles.

On the way down, I pass a vacant spot next to a man.

I'm so close to fainting that I just need to sit down. He turns out to be Danish and I say something about how crowded the boat is and try to give him a smile through the clotted blood on my face. He says something back to me and then we are quiet.

Sitting down doesn't help, I need to lie down or I will pass out. I get up from the seat and move towards Per.

Everybody is looking at me.

I can hardly walk straight.

"Per, I need to get down on the floor really fast, can you help me?"

My whole world has started to spin, I see thousands of black dots in front of my eyes and I don't hear anything.

I fall down among the life jackets on the floor. Per is in front of me, Anton and Axel are next to me.

A woman gives me something to drink and some crackers. I doze off from time to time during the 90-minute boat trip to Phuket.

Per looks out the window in the front of the boat. "I can see that we are approaching land; you need to get up from the floor soon. I think we are going to arrive in 15 minutes. I'll talk to the staff and ask if they can let injured people leave the boat first. I'll come back to help you, just stay where you are right now."

When he gets back, he bends down, and I put my arms around his neck to pull myself up.

My body has solidified even more while on the boat.

Together we walk through the aisle towards the stern of the boat, out through the doors. The heat and the sun strike our faces. As we pass the toilet doors, I'm about to faint.

I bend over a table to get my head down, but that doesn't help.
I lean over Per as he sits down but that doesn't help either.
I need to lie down, I know that, but there is not enough time
for me to get up from the floor again as my body is so stiff.
Looking ahead I notice a bench that some girls are sitting on.
"Per, please ask them if I may lay down on the bench. I can't
stand up anymore."
Anton and Axel look at me, I know that I'm acting very
strange.
My body has begun to protest.
To shut down.
I realize I'm in a very bad state.

As soon as Per walks towards the bench, I follow him and it´s
such a relief to lay down. Blood comes back up to my head and
I can hear again. A girl pours coca cola into my mouth. I close
my eyes; the sun is hot.
As soon as the boat docks at the quay, Per and a Thai man help
me up. They pave the way through the crowd.
There is no tent with "Sweden" on it, as I fantasized about all
night. But there are Thai ambulances.
Some nurses grab me and lead me to a stretcher. Everything is
happening very fast. The sudden sound of the stretcher makes
me jump, as it folds out in lying position.
The doors open and my stretcher is pushed into the
ambulance. It's cool, clean and nice. The doors close and the
ambulance sirens are turned on. We leave the harbor and it
feels like we're driving uphill. "Up is good, the wave might not
reach so high."
Per and the children sit next to a nurse, I let my eyes rest on
their faces.
In English, I repeat: "I'm allergic to penicillin. I'm allergic to
penicillin."

The Hospital

After about twenty minutes we arrive at the hospital. The
ambulance stops and the doors open.
A feeling of safety starts to emerge in me.
The second mission accomplished.
The nurses carry the stretcher through the emergency
entrance and take it straight into a large emergency room.
The stretcher is pushed up against the wall and in one second,
I am surrounded by doctors and nurses who start investigating
all the wounds on my body. They speak loud and fast in Thai.
One nurse tries to insert a needle into my hand, she pushes the
needle into my flesh the wrong way several times.
My clothes are taken off, my panties are stuck to coagulated
blood from the injuries to my lumbar spine and my buttocks.
Finally, I'm naked.
Everything hurts, as if the shock has kept the pain away for 24
hours and now every sensation is released. It feels like I'm
lying 3 feet above the stretcher and I'm screaming, screaming
out of pure pain.
The nurse who finally takes over the insertion of the needle in
my hand and manages to get it in, mentions morphine. "Yes...
please give me morphine, give me anything you can that takes
away the pain..."

After a while, the activities around me stop.
Everyone removes their hands from my body.
The doctor who has been concentrating on my hip injury says
in English that I need surgery. They roll my stretcher out from
the emergency room and past the children where they sit and
wait outside.
Our eyes meet on the way to the elevator, we smile at each
other.

The elevator stops and they rush me down the sloping ramps. I end up in a room with a surgeon, an anesthetist and two nurses.

"I'll take care of your injuries. I can do it with local anesthesia, but it's going to hurt so I would like to put you to sleep. Did you have breakfast today?" The surgeon has nice warm eyes.

Hmm... breakfast today?...

I try to picture a set table with coffee cups.

Have I seen that today?

Was it today the wave hit?

Or was it yesterday?

My memories are quickly flashing by.

"Last night at 3am I got five biscuits, and on the boat, I got some crackers. I have been drinking a lot."

Someone told me up in the emergency room that it can be dangerous to get sedated if you have eaten, this doesn't feel good.

"How long will it take?" I have made it this far; I can manage a while longer.

"It will take about an hour and a half."

Tears falls down my cheeks.

"We are going to put you to sleep." He smiles warmly towards me.

I get a mask over my mouth.

"Count down from 10."

I start counting 10, 9, 8, 7, when I reach 6, panic strikes. I rip the mask off my mouth. "You won't be able to sedate me. It is not working, not today. The morphine didn't help and now you will not be able to sedate me!" My voice is cracking.

His friendly face is close to mine.

"Keep counting. It will work, I promise."

When I reach 4 it happens, I sink into a welcoming liberating sleep. My body gets heavy and for the first time since the wave took me, I relax.

While I'm in surgery, they are taking care of Per's wound. The only injury he's got is one on his arm, and it's not deep.

It's a miracle that he wasn't more injured than that.

98

Per and the children receive a room at the hospital. We are so lucky. They don't separate us. We get to share a large room. After surgery, I stay a couple of hours in the recovery room. I'm vaguely aware of what is happening around me, I find myself in a dormant state and will stay so for the next few days.

Two nurses bring me to the room where Anton and Axel are waiting.

"Mamma..." Their voices are so smooth and soft, almost whispering.

"Hey..."

"How are you?" They carefully caress my hands.

"Why can't I open my eye? Is it swollen?"

"No, you have a bandage over your eyelid." Axel bends over my face and take a good look to see what the doctors have done to me. "You have bandages here on your cheek as well, where all the blood was before. You actually look really nice."

"Where is Dad?" He is not in the room.

"He is downstairs to get his medicine. Here at the hospital, he will be here soon and then we are going to buy some food."

I look around the room. It's big and nice, green and beige. A TV and private toilet, even a small balcony with a beautiful view. I see green treetops and a blue sky; we are clearly located on a hill. That feels good.

My bed is in the middle of the room. On my left side is a bed in grey plastic and on my right side there is a mattress and a cot for the children.

There is a drip hanging next to me and the nurses are checking my blood pressure repeatedly.

The nurses are so beautiful with their set hair and nice uniforms and strengthened little hats on their heads. You don't even hear when they are walking, it's like they move above the floor.

"Hey, how are you?" Per enters the room, in his hand he's got a bag with medicine.

"What time is it?"

"You've been away for three and a half hours. I talked to a doctor; you will need to stay here in the hospital for at least 4-5 days."

"What?" I was hoping that we would leave soon. As soon as I wake up properly so that we can continue – to do what? I know I have a plan, that I'm on a mission, but I don't remember what the next step is right now. But I will figure that out. We are going somewhere, and our goal was not Phuket. The wave came here too, I know that.

I will continue this discussion in a moment, when I can argue properly again, right now I just want to sleep.

I sink directly into the peaceful darkness that awaits around the corner.

Per and the children take a tuc tuc into the city to buy some food, chargers for Per's mobile, so that we can start communicating with the outside world as well as Gameboy for the children. Per's glasses disappeared in the wave, so the children have to help him find his way around the stores.

"Hello, Mom!" Two happy children wake me up. "Look what we bought, Gameboy. Check it out! And we bought food and drinks and yogurt. And we got lost all the time."

"Let me see?" I can't open my eyes completely, it's very comfortable being only half awake. The morphine is working. I am in a pleasant state between sleep and being awake.

Per and the children unpack the shopping bags. It is so amazing just to lie here, with closed eyes and listen to their voices.

He inserts the mobile charger into the wall. We receive so many text messages from worried people in Sweden. It is from family and close friends but also from unexpected persons. Per reads the messages out loud to us. Every message is so valuable.

He calls my dad. He's still in Florida. Dad is in shock, on the verge of panic, being so far away from us. I listen to their conversations and understand from Per's answers that my father has a thousand questions.

"What happened? Where did you go? How are the kids? How injured is Marie? What have they done to her? Where are you now? When are you coming home? How are you going to get home? Do you have money? How high was the wave? How did you get out of the wave? So, Marie has had surgery? How are the kids? Why didn't you tell me Marie was hurt? Do you all sleep at the hospital?"

They talk for a long time, there is a lot of things to talk about. A nurse enters our room with a cart of food for me. The hospital is vegetarian, not even coffee is served. The food is good and beats any hospital food in Sweden. I'm not hungry even though I haven't had any food since breakfast on the 26th. Per starts to feed me. It's stir-fried noodles with vegetables.

I eat a little but after a while I go to sleep again.

December 28th, 2004

My long hair is like a hard-tufted ball. It´s impossible to put my fingers through it, let alone a brush.

As I lie in bed with my head tilted to the side, I feel something hard in the back of my head that I have not felt before.

"Per, something hurts in the back of my head, what is it?"

"Something is stuck. Let me try to get it out."

He tries to get it out with his fingers. After a while, a piece of brick falls out.

"Was that brick stuck in my head? No wonder it hurts."

I have not been able to have my head on the pillow due to the pain I had. But at the same time; I can only lie on my back, so I have put a rolled-up towel under my neck.

"Can you please help me to wash my hair tomorrow, Per? It would be so nice to get rid of all the dirt and salt. Maybe you can buy some shampoo next time you buy food?"

"Do you really think you can stand up for that long? "

"It doesn't have to take a long time; I would be happy just to get rid of the worst dirt to start with."

Per's phone is ringing. It's my mother. He hands me the phone.

"Mom, hey..."

She doesn't say anything, she just cries. I hear her breathing and sobbing.

"Mom, it's okay now. Anton, Axel and Per are here with me. Everything's fine, Mom, and we'll be home soon."

Mom has talked to the Swedish Emergency Information several times. She has done everything she can to get us home as soon as possible.

It's strange, how you take turns being the strong one in relationships. When I hear my mother so sad, I become the strong and calm person.

A knock on our door, and in comes the ward round.

"Mom, the doctors are here. I will call you back as soon as they leave."

The doctor who's got the main responsibility for me, is such a humble kind man. After inspecting all my wounds, he explains that they need to cut open my stitches because the infection doesn't give in. I was on the island for such a long time, with open wounds, before I came to the hospital. On top of that it has been difficult for them to find the right medicine for me because of my allergy to penicillin. They have given me injections with antibiotics straight into my right hip and my doctor has discussed with Swedish doctors about alternative antibiotics that are strong enough, but they have not managed to stop the infections. So now they need to open some of my injuries again.

"Per, hold my hand. Anton and Axel, could you please stay outside the room just for a little while?"

There has been a lot of pain in the last 24 hours. I breathe through the pain while the doctor cuts up stitches from my hip and knee and presses out ulcer from the infected wounds.

Later that day, I get a call from my best friend Anette.

I cry, she is chattering teeth. We are feeling so many emotions at the same time.

"What happened?"

I share our story with her. She feels so far away, I miss her more than ever.

December 29th, 2004

My beautiful kind favorite nurse wakes me up in the morning.
She checks my blood pressure and temperature, smiles at me
and asks:
"Wash face?"
She wants to help me clean up. But is that really her
responsibility?
"Thank you, but my husband, he can wash me."
We smile at each other. She doesn't understand what I'm
saying. She helps me get out of bed. Slowly she leads me to the
bathroom and unbuttons my hospital gown.
Carefully she starts to wash me.
It feels so good to get a lukewarm soaped washcloth along my
back and my arms. Almost liberating. The last time I was in
water was three days ago and the water in the Tsunami was
filthy.
I see my naked body in the mirror.
I haven't looked at myself since I got here.
I've had surgery in nine different places all over my body and
face.
My body's turning blackish where I got the most beating.
My right arm is covered with dark bruises. The inside of my
arm is black and swollen. It's clear I didn't keep my arms close
to my body in the wave otherwise I wouldn't be this hurt.
My right leg is stiff, I look down to see that it's swollen, and
the color is black and blue.
My body looks so strange.
I find it hard to understand that it's my body I'm looking at.
All cleaned up and tucked in bed with new sheets, I feel like a
new person.
Per and the children return to the room with their breakfast.
Well, breakfast is perhaps to exaggerate because they eat the
same thing three times a day, white bread with tuna out of a
can. The only thing that is varied is the drink, sometimes juice
and sometimes yogurt.
"Per, I'm clean. The nurse helped me."

He bends down over me where I lie in bed and we kiss each other for the first time since the Tsunami.

It's not a kiss like any other kiss.

He smiles at me.
"Now we only have your hair left to take care of. I bought shampoo and conditioner."
He picks up his purchases, two conditioners, no shampoo.
"I'll go down to the store again and change after breakfast."
So, he does. But he returns with a shampoo for Asian hair – it's black. I'm bright blond, so that's not a good combination.
When he returns to the store for the third time, the staff smile at him.
"Third time's the charm, let's wash your hair."
He helps me up from the bed and pushing the drip stand next to me, we walk into the bathroom.
I bend over the basin as much as I possibly can.
The water that runs through my hair turns brown from the dirt.
He finds such strange things. Pieces of bark, stones, long black plastic straws. Where the item's been stuck, there are wounds in my scalp.
I look at the items.
Where did the wave take me?
What has happened to my head?
Back in bed, I feel born-again.
The amazing feeling of being clean.
Imagine that something so ordinary can be such a pleasure.

Anton and Axel are on the floor below us, where there are other injured Swedes. They go down there every now and then during the day to keep them company. Per and I are watching the news on CNN and Thai TV. The local channel broadcasts uncomfortably realistic reports from the Tsunami, so many dead bodies, that we don't watch that channel when the kids are here. But we do turn it on as soon as they leave the room. It´s like we don't understand that what we are looking at has really happened and that we were right there when it did. We know that we are in Thailand and we know it has happened, but we still have the feeling that everything we see is happening far, far away.

Suddenly in the middle of the news, the TV shuts down and the air conditioning stops.

The power's gone at the hospital.

The sound of a child running as fast as he can outside our room.

It's Anton and he's terrified.

His heart beats so violently that I can see it through his t-shirt. He's face is pale.

"What is it, Anton? It's nothing dangerous. It's just a power failure, it will be on soon."

"Mom, this is how it started in Kao Lak. The power went out and then the wave hit!" He speaks so fast, with panic and fear in his voice.

"But Anton, we are far from the ocean and we are high up on a hill. If there's another wave, it won't reach us up here, I promise you."

He sits on my bed, I reach for his hand, it's wet.

"I promise Anton, we are safe up here, I promise you!"

"Mom, when can we go home to Sweden? I don't want to be here anymore!"

"We will certainly be home on New Year's Eve and that's in three days. Dad's talking to International SOS. He spoke to their boss and there is a plane in two days, and we are going home in that plane. And until we leave, we are safe here."

He crawls up in bed with me and I put my arm around him. We lie there, side by side, quiet, for a long time.

"I will go downstairs again. Mom, are you sure the wave won't come here?"

"Anton, I'm sure there won't be another wave now. And yes, we are high, high up on a hill."

As the door closes behind him, I fall into a deep sleep. I am so tired. My body is exhausted. Even when I manage to relax mentally, my body doesn't. It's stiff, hard and sore. My back is tight. It feels like I have a stick along my spine. I have a hard time moving and it hurts everywhere and all the time. Except when I sleep. That's where I get some peace.

First meeting with Sweden

We are sleeping. It's the middle of the night.
The door to our room suddenly opens with a bang, and several persons storm in.
The bright light in the ceiling is turned on.
Dizzy and stressed by their dramatic entrance, we just stare at them.
"Who's the patient here?" A tall, thin Swedish man calls out his question at the same time he sees the drip attached to my arm. He starts asking questions like an automatic rifle spitting out bullets.
"What happened? What have they done?"
"Tsunami, operation."
"Are you x-rayed?"
"Uh...I don't know."
"You can have internal bleeding, it's dangerous, you can die, does it hurt when I put pressure on your stomach?"
He frightens me, he is so stressed.
He rips off my blanket, puts his hands on my hip bones and press down.
"Ouch!! It hurts, I just had surgery." I breathe heavily from the pain he is causing. "Please, be gentle." I whisper between my teeth.
"Does it hurt here?" He touches my stomach.
It has the size of a balloon after all these days on drip.
I whisper between my heavy breaths. "Who are you??"
"I'm from the National Board of Health and Welfare."
"National Board of Health and Welfare???" Per stands next to my bed.
"We're going to bring injured people to Sweden."
"We have already solved that. I have been in contact with International SOS since December 27th. We were supposed to leave today but apparently that plane went to Norway instead. The plan is to leave tomorrow. We are going to fly to Kastrup in Copenhagen as we live in Malmo, in the south of Sweden."
"No. We'll take over from now."

"What? Take over? We are a registered case at the SOS, are they informed about this? That you suddenly take over?" Per is getting annoyed.

The tall man from the National Board of Health and Welfare looks at a woman who works as something with ambulances, their presentations are as quick as his questions.

"How do we proceed with this?" He asks her.

"Have you received a case number from SOS? We are giving you a case number from us as well. If you do not show up, you don't."

She writes the number 204 on my arm with an ink pen.

I look at my number on my arm and then back at her.

"Shouldn't we tell you if we don't come? Don't you need to know that?"

"Well of course, that might be good." She writes down her cell phone number on a piece of paper.

Then they disappear as fast as they came. Per and I look at each other.

"What happened? What was decided?" I am so confused.

Per spends the rest of the night on his mobile, talking to different people at SOS to get some clarity.

We doze off in the morning, still not knowing what's going to happen. It feels like we have become a brick in a political game of bringing home injured Swedes. We had everything under control but now it's completely upside down and it doesn't seem like SOS has any say anymore.

December 31st, 2004 – No. 204 is going home

We still believe that we have arranged everything ourselves and we have informed our families, so they know what's going to happen. We are going to arrive at Copenhagen, Kastrup airport, and that is very important, I do NOT want to end up in Stockholm. Far from where we live.
We need to come home.

As they wake us up at 7 o'clock in the morning we understand that something is about to happen. Our flight with SOS does not leave until this afternoon.
Per assist the children with their clothes. I struggle, still having the drip, wearing the hospital gown and no underwear. Per tries his best to get me out of what I'm wearing and put some new clothes on. As I walk around, blood leaks out from the drip needle. I feel nauseous and dizzy watching my blood leaving my body.
"Per, I don't know what to do...?"
"Let me call for a nurse. I don't know if you're going to keep the drip or not."
The nurse grabs the needle and pulls it out of my hand and puts a bandage over. I see my blood crawling through the bandage. There is so much stress in the air, my heart is beating hard.
A nurse helps me to get dressed. We are ready but nothing happens for a long time. We' are waiting, but we don't know what's going to happen.
Suddenly the door opens and three people in hospital uniform grab my bed and rolls me out from the room, down to the entrance level into a waiting ambulance.
We leave the hospital and head for Phuket Airport.
The ambulance stops at a huge hangar. Doctors and nurses are waiting for us. They lay me down on a stretcher on the floor and a Swedish nurse sits down by my side.

I don't know what we talk about but in the middle of a sentence she mentions something about our flight taking us to Stockholm.

Like a flash from the sky, without warning, it hits me right in my heart.

I start to vent and cry. I get a panic attack.

"I don't want to go to Stockholm!!"

My body is shaking. I am angry.

I try to take deep breaths.

Try to calm down.

Per lets the nurse know that we are taken care of by SOS and that our plane is flying to Copenhagen.

"But... There will probably not be an SOS plane to Copenhagen today. If you want, you can wait and see, but chances are you won't be leaving today then. It's your choice."

"Choose between what? You're telling me we probably don't have much of a choice??"

They put us in a smaller room. There are not that many people here. Water bottles are handed out, fruit and T-shirts.

A Swedish nurse is by my side.

Anton and Axel are next to me. We don't talk much; their eyes wander around the room.

Wounded persons. Lonely sad children, injured adults crying... It's a sad place.

Per talks on his mobile basically nonstop. He talks to SOS, my dad, SOS again...

I recognize a man from Malmo. He is a journalist at Sydsvenskan, our main daily newspaper. We don't know each other very well, but we have met briefly. As soon as he sees me, he comes over to me.

"No...is that really you Marie... Shit, I barely recognize you. How are you??"

He kneels on the floor by my side, takes my hand and we start talking... and we talk, and talk and talk...

We receive the information that the boarding will start soon with injured people.

We are booked on the first plane to Sweden.

To Stockholm, but I am okay with that now.

I realize that my strong reaction had do to with the feeling of not being able to predict what's going on.

I need to know what is going to happen so that I can prepare myself.

That's all.

Military stretchers are brought into the room. They have thick green fabric between the heavy steel edges. A stretcher is placed next to my mattress and they lift me onto it. Several straps are attached over my body before I am lifted and carried out from the hangar.

Per and the kids walk next to me.

Out in the sun, the heat is incredible.

A large car with lifting devices waits for us. My stretcher is placed on "mechanic arms" and I'm elevated in the air. I close my eyes tight and hold my arms close to my body.

After a while, the car is loaded with 3 stretchers with patients and the car drives slowly out to the aircraft.

The air-stair is steep and narrow. I understand it's not easy to bring up the stretchers. If I'd been able to, I'd help them, but I just lie there scared and tense as they slowly carry me up into the plane.

It's nice and cool inside the plane. The staff is Scandinavian and amazing. The pilot has warm kind eyes, I immediately feel safe.

The plane has been rebuilt to fit the stretchers. At the front there are 5 rows of seats left, the rest of the plane is rebuilt. Stretchers are placed in rows, three by three on top of each other like narrow bunk beds. My stretcher is placed in the middle, I will get one person below me and another person 20 inches above me.

Anton, Per and Axel are sitting on the row in front of me, I don't take my eyes off them. Their fear and tension have begun to fade away. From the hangar we could see the ocean through the windows and that was terrifying for them. Being so close to the water again. Their bodies were tense, and their eyes were staring out through the windows.

A vague feeling of safety is surrounding us now, here in the plane.

I'm beginning to see the end of the mission that started when I climbed out from the helicopter on Phi Phi Island.

It takes time to fill the plane, stretcher by stretcher. They give us water to stay hydrated and the children have their hands full of Marabou chocolates. We have a 24-hour flight ahead of us, so I try to relax and settle in on the stretcher.

My stomach is the size of a football after many days on drip feeding and I need to go to the bathroom really bad.

A nurse gives me something white in plastic to pee in. They hang up blankets in front of my stretcher to give me some privacy.

Have you ever tried to pee lying down?

I can tell you, it's hard. Impossible I would say.

"You need to relax." The nurse is kind, but her advice doesn't help.

Per tries to help me, he puts some pressure on my stomach, trying to help me let go and release... nothing helps.

"You need to try harder, Marie."

"Per, I am relaxed every night when I lie in bed, but I never pee! Since you are a small child, that's exactly what you are taught – to relax WITHOUT peeing in bed!"

It's not fair, I know, but I'm getting irritated. And worried. I need to find a solution to this! I'm stuck here for at least 24 hours so I need to learn how to go to the bathroom laying down. I have been instructed to drink a lot in addition, so it will be quite a large number of times that I need to go to the bathroom during the flight.

Finally, after a long struggle to "relax" without success, I give up. It's just not going to happen.

"So, what's your plan?" Per is irritated and he doesn't try to hide it. "You are aware that we will be on this plane for the next 24 hours, right?"

"I know. I have a plan. I need to get up on my feet and walk to the bathroom. Can you ask the doctor over there to help us? I need the two of you to assist me."

The three of us discuss how to proceed. The stretcher has a metal frame and I lie sunken down on fabric in between so it's "upsloping". I will have to get my body over that frame and that's the problem. And as I have another stretcher over me, I can't sit up straight on my stretcher, I need to crawl myself out.

The doctor promises me that my injuries that are stitched will not tear up.

"Ok, let's go!" I'm fully focused on my task.

Per and the doctor get on their knees below my stretcher and I start to crawl up the metal frame. I take deep breaths, flex my body, focus and bite my tongue. This is it. I am going to get out of here. I gather all the power and energy that I have in my body. My scream of pain remains silent.

I push my body over the frame, down on their backs and up on my feet like I have done nothing else my entire life.

My head is spinning, I have double vision, but I don't care!

I made it! Now I know the journey that lies ahead is going to be fine.

On my way back from an amazingly wonderful visit to the bathroom, I stop at Anton and Axel's seats. They look so happy.

The pilot has left the door open to the cockpit and told the children that they are welcome. Both Anton and Axel thought it was amazing.

The staff and their way of caring for us is a memory for the rest of our lives. You were so important to us right then and there and you couldn't have done it in a better way. Thank you, thank you, thank you...

I get back onto my stretcher again. The straps are tightened by a man who also helps me with the seat belt, which got a huge buckle that rests heavily on my stomach.

After two and a half hours, the plane is loaded with injured people and relatives and ready to take off.

When the plane leaves Thailand, tears are falling. The silence in the plane is solid.

The flight back home

As soon as the plane reaches, a certain altitude, we get some information. That we have a long flight ahead of us but there is plenty of food and water onboard, so please just reach out if we need anything. During the flight we are going to have three short landings, to throw out trash and refuel the plane.

The doctors start working with the injured. One by one, they go through our bodies. Examine our wounds, disinfect, and put on new bandages.

Axel and Anton come to me every now and then to make sure everything is fine with me. They put their hands on my forehead, caresses my hand and arm.

"How are you, Mom?"

"I'm fine, how are you?"

"Great! We get as much chocolate as we want and coca cola too!"

"Can you believe it? We are on our way home! Doesn't it feel good?" They both nod and look relieved.

When it's my turn to be examined, the doctor asks me to share what has happened as he starts investigating my injuries. Bandage after bandage is removed and the wounds are inspected.

"You have received really good care. It looks very good."

Food and drinks are being served to the passengers, I lie on my stretcher, just listening. Looking around.

There is a strong sense of sharing and caring on the plane, almost like it was in the jungle. It is impossible to describe the atmosphere on board. Sadness, loss, pain, uncertainty, and fear mixed with respect, security, kindness and skilled staff.

I can see Anton and Axel's profiles from my stretcher.

I hear their voices and it's like cotton to my soul.

Many people start talking to each other and I can hear Anton and Axel, for the first time, telling their story to a young couple sitting on the other side of the aisle. As I listen, a warm feeling of gratitude fills me. After a while, the children's story has shifted to funny memories of other events in their lives.
The couple laugh and the children continue to share.

I didn't tell you on the plane, so I'm writing it now. Thank you for taking the time to listen to my children in the midst of your destiny!
You did an amazing thing!

The first landing is Deli, India. It's dark outside and we go straight to a fuel station, we're not among the other planes. Per takes the opportunity to call my father to inform him where we are and where we are going. Dad has talked to SOS and been told that I am still on their list of passengers who are leaving Thailand.
I get the phone, we cry a bit, both dad and me.
"You're on your way now, Marie! You're on your way home!!"
"I've talked to a therapist who can help you when you get home. We're going to fix this, Marie."

We leave India, the next stop is the United Arab Emirate. There is silence on the plane. Most people are asleep. I can't sleep. After about an hour, I ask a nurse for an aspirin to reduce the pain. While waiting for it to start working, I look out the window, into the night. My thoughts and feelings are confused and messy. I cry quietly not to disturb anyone.
A nurse notices my tears and gets down on her knees by my stretcher. She takes my hand, and we start talking.
I tell her that I'm worried about a thing I read in a tabloid that's been circulating on the plane. It was an article about us patients being isolated in hospital when we arrive in Sweden. Where would I end up then? Stockholm far away, from where we live? And where would Per and the children go?
I cannot be separated from Anton and Axel.
I need to be close to them.

She assures me that no one is going to split us up, that we will be together no matter what. We talk for a long time.

It's a nice conversation that settles me.

We fly through New Year's Eve twice that night. No one wishes Happy New Year. People are either sleeping through the night or wrapped up in their own thoughts. We begin the new year, strapped to stretchers on an airplane from Thailand. Some of us with all family members, others with grief and sadness and loss of a loved one. We all left Sweden just a little while ago. We were all on our dream trip. None of us could have imagined what was going to happen.

Life is so unpredictable. That is clearer than ever.

Next stop. Garbage is carried out and the plane is refueled. It's pitch black in the middle of the night. We take off for the final flight, to Turkey. Everyone seems to be asleep on the plane but I'm cold and my body refuses to relax. A nurse puts another blanket on me, and I get a sleeping pill. I fall asleep after a while.

Next time I wake up is when we are about to land at Arlanda airport in Stockholm, Sweden...

Sweden

It´s only 4.30am when we touch ground.

The plane drives a long way towards large hangars. When we approach, gates open and the plane is steered in. It's an enormous place with cold bright lighting. The doors of the plane open and we are informed that those who can walk should get out of the plane first so that the stretchers can be carried out, one by one.

I entered first on the plane and will be carried out among the last. Time passes, every stretcher takes a long time.

It's chilly so additional blankets are being handed out.

Someone says something, I do not really know what, but something that makes me concerned. "Where are Anton, Per and Axel?"

"They're not here."

"Not here?? You promised we wouldn't be separated! Aren't they outside the plane??!!"

"No."

My body starts shaking, tears run down my face and I get terribly angry.

My seatbelt and straps hold me down in a firm grip, I can't move, I can't get loose, I can't look for them.

I'm totally dependent on others and I hate the feeling.

I need to be in control right now.

I need to know that my children are close.

I scream in pure despair.

"You promised me this would not happen!! I asked you what would happen here at Arlanda because I NEEDED to know! This is the ONLY thing that matters to me, nothing else!!"

"We are going to find your family right away, I promise! We're going to find them and make sure they get here."

A doctor has his arms around me, holding me tight to calm me down. A nurse is in front of me. She looks right into my eyes.

"We informed the staff that this should not happen here at Arlanda. I don't understand how this could happen Marie and I understand why you are worried."

I take a few deep breaths, calm down and decide to trust them. It's time for my stretcher to leave the plane now, it's unloaded from the steel device and a number of men start carrying me through the plane, down the narrow steep aisle.

I ask the doctor if anyone can force me to go to a hospital. He looks at me with a warm smile. "You're in charge now... I know what I would have done in your situation." I know exactly what to do.

The light is dazzling when I get down on the ground and my stretcher is placed on the concrete floor. I feel the coldness through the fabric of the stretcher.
A fireman kneels by my side. "How are you doing?"
"I'm okay. I just want my family; I don't know where they are."
"They'll be here soon; I think they are at the crisis center inside the airport."
"Do you know where we're going now? Where are they going to take us? "
"I don't know anything. Are you going to Gothenburg?"
"No, we're going to Malmo. Or Copenhagen."
"I'll see what I can find out, I've just heard that there will be flights to Gothenburg, nothing else."
He walks away, I close my eyes and pull the blankets close to my body. A nurse comes up and puts a pair of thick socks on my bare feet.
After a few moments I hear:
"Mom, we are here!!" Anton and Axel comes running towards me. Each with a cuddly animal and chocolate from the crisis center.
I pull their faces close to mine and breath in their scents.
I can't stand not knowing where they are.

Then everything happens fast. A small ambulance flight is heated up to take the four of us to Malmo. Two pilots and a nurse await us.
We take off, up through the clouds. The sky is so beautiful. Clouds as soft as cotton beneath us. The sun starts to rise, the sky has all the shades of pink.

They open a thermos with coffee, it smells wonderful. Cookies are also available; the children eat their chocolate bars and share some with the pilot. After a while, both children are sound asleep.

When we land, an ambulance is waiting for me and a taxi for Per and the children.

A nurse sits by my side in the ambulance.

"I'm not going to the hospital."

"No?"

"No."

"So.... Where are you going?"

"Home. I am going home. I promise I'll go to the hospital tomorrow, but right now I'm going home."

From my stretcher I can see rooftops that I recognize. We are approaching our home. It's close now. I know exactly where we are, and I know that right now we are driving into our street and RIGHT NOW WE STOP OUTSIDE OUR HOUSE!

The doors open and they begin to carry out my stretcher. At that very moment my mother walks out from our house.

My mother.

My mom.

She is wearing her black winter coat and a white cap over her bright hair.

She leans over me on the stretcher and starts crying She hugs me hard and tears run down her cheeks.

I breath her scent and whisper. "Mom...Mom...."

I don't cry.

The air smells like winter.

My children are here, next to me.

The sun is shining, and the sky is blue.

I see my home and I have my mother's arms are around me.

For me, everything is fine now, this was my goal. This is what I've been fighting for, my mission since I left the helicopter at Phi Phi Island.

We are home.

Mission completed.

Coming home

"You are so wounded, Marie. " Mom is bent over the stretcher, she examines every inch of my face.
After a while she wipes her tears, caresses my cheeks and smiles at the paramedics who's holding my stretcher.
As they pull out my stretcher, she is right by my side.
Our neighbors are running out on the street in their socks, everyone is crying. Hugging us. Many things are being said, I don't remember what they are saying. But I do begin to realize how life has been here for them at home having us so far away.
Per, me and the children look around us with big, amazed eyes.
Two worlds meet at this moment here on our street.
Our world, a world we have not grasped yet, and the world here at home where they have been fed with information from the media.
The paramedics, who throughout this scene of powerful emotions have watched everything with me lying on the stretcher, seem to be as touched by the moment as we are.
"I think I can walk through the gate by myself. You don't have to carry me."
"Are you sure?"
"Yes, thanks for all your help, I'll be fine from now on."
Per helps me rise from the stretcher. I stand there in the middle of our street. Wearing pink Thai nighties and sore feet in sandals. I am as confused as I look.
Mom's holding my arm in a firm grip as we go through the gate, into our house. Everything is as it always has been. The universe hasn't been knocked out here.
We have received beautiful flowers from friends, customers and colleagues. Beautiful bouquets with the most wonderfully written cards. It brings as much warmth to our home as a bonfire on a late winter night.
The first thing I see when I enter the living room is a tabloid with photos of missing Swedish children.

Two of the children are children we were supposed to meet up with in Thailand a couple of days after the Tsunami hit.
Now they are missing.
It feels like someone just pulled a black garbage bag over my head.
I have not understood the extent of what happened, or maybe I did, but I didn't want to let it sink in.
Death enters my mind, it's pitch black and it's terrible.
I realize more and more the extent of the blessing of the four of us surviving.
Now when we are in safety, I slowly take in how close we were to a terrible ending.

Mom is close to me all the time; she offloads some responsibilities from Per so he can get some rest.
She helps me when I want to lie down on the couch, she tucks me in at night, she fluffs the pillows behind my neck, she brings me water, she caresses my face, she just looks at me, she hugs me... she sees me.
I have never seen her like this.
Anton logs on to Luna storm. Axel runs up to his room and back down the stairs again.
"Mom, I want us to have a lot of people here today." I see Anton's back and I hear his fingers tapping the keyboard.
"Would you like something to eat? Should I make coffee? Are you okay, Marie?" Mom has the energy level of a five-year-old on a birthday party. She is running between the four of us, touching us to make sure that we are, really are, here.
"We have to call Per-Ola (my brother), he wanted to come here to."
Per-Ola arrives within ten minutes. He lays beside me on the couch and wets my whole face with tears. I am still not crying. Everything is good. But I do sense his fear, and that is a scary feeling.
My half-sister calls, cries and asks if she can come – she walks through the door one hour later with a bouquet of flowers. She is crying, hugging me, I understand that she was convinced we had died because she knew Phi Phi Island was hit hard by the Tsunami.

"But how did you know we were at Phi Phi Island when the wave hit?"
"Marie, you wrote that in your last text message. The Christmas greeting message?"
Oh. The text message I sent to so many persons. I forgot about that.

Dad's partner Lena works within health care in Sweden and as I haven't yet been tested for the germs they write about in the tabloids; we cannot meet indoors. With red roses and tears we meet on the terrace. We cry and talk. I feel the fear they have felt.
Later that evening, tears start rolling down my cheeks. I lie alone on the couch in the living room. Candle lights gently softens the room as emotions flow through me; feeling safe, grateful to be alive, realizing for the first time the numbers of lives that no longer exist, our missing friends and their missing children, that in this very moment people are screaming out their grief for a child or a husband – everything hits me and the tears are as liberating as a spring flood.
Mom hears and comes to me. She lies down by my side on the couch. Side by side, hand in hand, we cry. She and I.
Around 10pm we are exhausted. Mom helps me up off the couch and up the stairs to the upper floor. She stands by my side as I brush my teeth, follows me into the bedroom, fluffs my pillows and lifts off the duvet.
"Will you be able to sleep Marie?"
"Yes, I think so, I'm so tired."
"If you can't, just come down and wake me up."
"Can you please help me to my bed?"
I put my arm around her neck and together we slowly lay down my body into my bed. She puts a big pillow under my right leg and the duvet on top of me. My stiff body weighs a ton, at least.
I fall asleep before she has left the bedroom.
During the night, Anton and Axel come into our beds.

I wake up with their bodies by my side, not close though, as they don't want to risk touching my injuries. It's still dark outside, I have no idea what time it is, but I don't believe it's time to get up yet.

"Mom, are you awake?" Axel whispers in the dark. He sounds alert.

"Yes, I'm awake. Have you had a good night's sleep?"

"Mom, I'm awake too," Anton says.

"You sound awake, do you think its morning?"

"I think so because I'm a little hungry."

We stay in bed and whisper to each other for a while.

"What do you say, should we get up?"

"Can we? It's all dark outside."

"Of course, we can! We can do whatever we want!"

We are very quiet not to wake Per up who sleeps deeply. He needs all the rest he can get. At the hospital in Thailand I needed help with adjusting my bed regularly, even throughout the nights, as my back was so much in pain. So, Per didn't get much sleep. I can see how exhausted he is.

They help me down the stairs. Sune, our dog, comes running towards us with a wagging tail, he's very happy to see us.

I look at the clock in the kitchen, It´s 5:30am. We wake up my mom. She is almost as happy today as she was yesterday when we got home.

"Are you up already?"

"I figured it out, we are on Thai time, that's why we woke up so early."

Anton helps me when I need to lie down on the couch after a while.

Mom lights candles everywhere, in the kitchen, in the living room. The soft glow is golden and warm. I smell the scent of coffee from the kitchen.

"Mom, can't we always be on Thai time? Then we never have to hurry in the morning anymore." Axel joins me on the couch.

Later that day Per returns from grocery shopping with 'Sydsvenskan' and 'Skanska Dagbladet', the two largest daily newspapers in our part of Sweden. Photos of us from the airport in Thailand on the frontpage. "No. 204 is going home" is the headline.
I read my own words in the article over and over again, it almost becomes a mantra. There is one sentence from the article that keeps repeating in my mind:

"Her words leave her mouth, but love does not leave the room for a second"

There is something with that sentence that touches me in a very deep way. That brings tears to my eyes.
If the journalist Joakim could feel my love for my children in the midst of the chaos, then maybe I was not such a disaster as a mother as I believed.
If Joakim could sense my love, surely my children must have felt it too?
I live with a strong feeling of guilt. Guilt, over the fact that I wasn't a present parent. That I didn't hug Anton when we met on the ground for the first time after the wave.
The words in the article soothes my heart and soul.
They give me comfort, they heal.
A team from 'Cold Facts' a TV program on Channel 4, comes to our house for an interview. The journalist is also named Joakim just as Joakim from 'Sydsvenskan' he has a pleasant, soft and warm personality. It might sound strange, but the meetings with these two persons, is the start of the healing process for us.

The hospital in Malmo

I got all the medication that I need, on a daily basis, from the hospital in Thailand. But I promised the doctor on the airplane to Sweden that I would go to the hospital in Malmo for tests and a check-up, so we did, Per and I.

My main purpose of the visit is Anton and Axel. I want to discuss how we can help them heal from what they have been through. As Per and I are affected by the same trauma, the four of us are going to need professional help. The sooner the better.

I wear my pink Thai pants and a t-shirt. Sandals on my feet as the wounds are far from healed making it impossible to wear shoes. My feet are still yellow from iodine.

Per helps me out of the car by leaning forward so that I get hold of his neck and slowly, slowly pull myself out of the car. It hurts. A lot.

There is a special entrance due to bacteria from foreign hospitals. We are going to be tested. We walk into the hospital. It's just the two of us here. Its empty and deserted. After a few minutes, a nurse shows us into a room and asks me to take off my clothes.

After a while I stand there, in the middle of the room, naked. My body is covered by bandages and yellow iodine stains and big black bruises. It's cold in the room, I'm freezing. My head starts spinning, I am about to faint from sitting and standing up for too long. I need to lie down.

Per helps me down on the hospital bed and the nurse puts a sheet over me. It feels like she is avoiding looking at my body. "The doctor will be here soon." She closes the door behind her as she leaves the room.

An older female doctor comes into the room. She and a nurse look at my injuries in silence. They don't ask me anything. There is a strange atmosphere in the room.

After a while, she asks us if we want to meet a counselor. Yes. That's exactly what we want. Let's talk about how we're going to take care of Anton and Axel.

Per helps me get dressed and a counselor enters the room after a while. She shakes our hands and informs us where we can find different contact numbers. Before she leaves the room, she says: "And if you feel really bad, you can call the psychiatric emergency..."

No one asks how we are.

How our children are doing.

What happened to us.

I refuse to go back there again.

Maria, a good friend of mine who is working as a nurse at the local medical group, helps me to get in touch with a doctor called Christer. Meeting him and his amazing nurses is medicine for both body and soul.

Per and I join a POSOM group for others in our situation. I'm part of this group for a long time. It becomes a safe place for sharing and listening.

We also start to go regularly to a therapist. I read somewhere that parents with seriously sick children, either get a divorce in the end or an even stronger marriage. Rarely something in between. I understand the reason behind that now. In a crisis you become vulnerable, there is no energy left to play games or hide your feelings.

The relationship is there in front of us, as it is.

Naked.

A couple of weeks after we came home my father visited for a cup of coffee. As he said goodbye, he turns to me. "Marie, after this experience, you will never get a divorce."

Right then and there I realize that Per and I are at a crossroad. Both in regards to our lives and our marriage.

We are so different as persons and that might become a huge problem as we are going to heal and deal with this in different ways going forward.

I went up back to the living room.

" Per, I am going to act in weird ways over the years to come. I will cry when you don't understand why, I am going to be afraid when you don't see a reason to and I am going to need to talk about the same things over and over again. Please never stop me. Let me do this my way, and I will let you do this your way. Let's make sure we support each other."
Not once did he make fun of me.
Not once over the years to come did he make me feel stupid or odd.
Even if he did not always understand me.
Our marriage survived the crisis.
We worked our way through it.
I would say we came out stronger on the other side.
As man and woman, as mother and father, as friends.

I find a support group for Anton and Axel. It's only them and two other girls. They don't like it, but I make them go until summer. That was the only help they got.
I reached out to the trauma unit for children at the hospital but was told that my children's experiences were not terrible enough for that unit.
I didn't know how to proceed.
What did she know after a few minutes on the phone?
Why didn't I fight more?
Why did I give up?
A few years later, being exposed to natural disasters are included on the list to help children with their trauma in that particular unit at the hospital.

January 9th 2005– in the middle of the night

During travel planning, did we ever have a plan where we did not stay on Phi Phi Island December 26th?
We changed our trip several times during the planning phase, added and removed islands. Changed the number of nights on the different islands during the three week long vacation and island hopping.
Did we ever have a plan that did not include Phi Phi the 26th?
In the middle of the night the 9th of January that questions keep me awake.
 I need to know.
I get out of bed and down the stairs to turn on the computer to read all the email sent between me and the travel agencies.
There are at least fifty emails but finally I find what I'm looking for – no matter how much I changed the plans – we were always on Phi Phi Island on December 26th...

Mom leaving and school starting

Mom needs to go home as her work as a teacher starts in two days when the Christmas break is over. She lives in Ahus, a 90 minute drive from us.

I can't believe I had to turn forty to fully realize how important parents are, even when you are grown up. Her presence has been priceless.

I spend all my energy on being a present mother to Anton and Axel. Mom did exactly that for me. She made space for me to let go, a place where I didn't have to be strong. She protected me and looked after me the same way I am trying to do for my children.

Before she leaves, she holds me for a long time.

"Marie, I see how you want to give the world to your sons. But at some point, you need to be able to say no again." She smiles and caress my cheek. I know what she means. My answer to everything they have wanted since we came home has been Yes. Yes, you may stay up a little longer before you go to bed. Yes, you may have ice cream today as well.

No is not part of my vocabulary just yet.

The principal of Anton's and Axel´s school, Anna-Karin, contacted my father while we were still in Thailand. She knew that we were on vacation in Thailand because of the leave application form we had submitted, where I noted my father as a close relative.

They have asked us for a meeting with the teachers before the school starts. They want us to share what has happened and want to know how Anton and Axel are doing.

My father and I have a very emotional meeting with them. Anna-Karin is amazing, and Anton's teacher tells us with tears running that when the principal called her to let her know that Anton survived, she screamed. "Go Anton!!"

I leave the school with a very good feeling.

Our children are going to be well taken care of in school.

Thoughts that flows freely

I don't want to spend any time on superficial relationships.
The conversations feel forced, leaving me drained of energy.
Meeting people I have deep relationships with is soft and
warm as cotton.
The difference is huge.

I have also thought a lot about Per's strength.
It strikes me as astonishing.
I remember the morning it hit me. The first time I realized
that Per could have died.
He walks down the stairs and I am in our kitchen.
I turn around and look at him and the awareness hits me right
in my stomach.
My God... he could have died!
I put my arms around him, and we hold each other for a long,
long time....
I had so much faith in him, in his power and strength that in
my mind he was immortal. That's why, just before the wave
hits, I scream to him, even though he's in exactly the same
situation as I am, that he needs to take care of the kids.
That was my true belief, I was so sure he would make it, no
matter what was in line for us.

The first month I am on sick leave full time and Per half-time.
We have breakfast with the children before they leave for
school every morning and then we place ourselves in front of
the computer. We spend hours surfing the internet, searching
for anything and everything that might give us information
about what happened. It's almost addictive. It's like a puzzle
but we don't know what the picture should look like or when
we are finished.

I wear the same clothes every day, I wash them in the evenings to dry during the night. It's either my green Thai pants that Per helped me put on up in the jungle or the pink pants from the hospital. Anton and Axel find it a bit embarrassing when their friends come visiting after school and I'm dressed like that, but I really want to wear these clothes. Just the same way I only use the shampoo from the hospital in Thailand when I wash my hair. When the bottle is getting empty, I put it aside with some shampoo still left. I don't want to throw the bottle away.

My whole self, all that's me has not returned from Thailand – not yet – I will return soon, but before I do, I need to wear my Thai clothes and I want the same scent in my hair as I had in the hospital.

When I feel whole again – I will throw away the shampoo bottle and put my Thai clothes away.

I try to go for a short walk every day to get my body going. I always walk past the children's school. Either to see them playing in the school yard or to look into their classrooms. Yes, they are here.

I still have them.

January 2nd, 2005

Anton skips up the stairs.
"Anton, you seem so happy!"
It's wonderful to see him like this.
"Of course, I'm happy – we survived! All four of us!"

January 25th, 2005

"Mom, just imagine how many children who will never celebrate their birthdays again."
Axel and I lie in his bed.
"Yes, it is terrible, Axel. It's so sad."
"I hope I'll never get shot, Mom"
"Well, why would you get shot?" I don't understand what he's talking about, why he says that.
"Why not? There are so many children who died in the Tsunami, and they didn't know of that before."
I hold him tight next to me and breathe in his scent, I fill my lungs with him.

End of January 2005

It's morning, the kids are at school and outside it's cold. The sky is grey.

I'm home by myself for the first time and I play Marie Fredriksson's new CD "The Change". Something happens inside me when I hear the music, she sings about life and death and the struggle in between. The music goes straight into my heart, right into my soul. "Thank God I ´m alive"... my tears flow down my cheeks.

Thank God the kids made it...

Thank God Per made it...

Thank God I'm alive...

I was worried about being alone for the first time and now that I am swept away by the emotional hurricane I first become completely stiff and feel the need to call someone, someone who can save me from my loneliness and my own feelings. The music fills the living room, I lie down on the couch under a blanket and just listen and feel.

It's not dangerous. It's not dangerous, let it come.

Nasty dark thoughts grab me by my throat.

Death. So close.

Gratitude that we survived.

All the suffering, the grief, memories of all of those that died.

Powerful emotions.

Gratitude and grief, almost each other's opposites.

Black and white, I realize that the ocean of emotions is grey, and it is large, and it is stormy and horrendous in its power. It's right here in front of me and the only way to get to the other side – is to swim through with full force, there are no shortcuts, and a life jacket would only delay it.

I throw myself straight into the sea of emotions and start swimming...

March 11th, 2005

Per, Axel and I lie in Axel's bed saying good night, which often takes a while nowadays. Many thoughts appear in the dark when we are close to each other. I'm in the middle of the bed, with Per on one side and Axel on the other side.
"What if you had died, Mom, then dad and I would have been lying here all alone."
"Yes, you would, Axel."
He reflects for a minute or two.
"Dad, you wouldn't marry someone else, would you?"
Before Per answers, I respond: "I hope that if I had died in Thailand, dad would one day find someone that both you and he liked and that he would marry her."
Axel is quiet again, thinking.
"Well.... of course, if you're dead, mom, you wouldn't have any feelings anyway."

March 16th, 2005

I surf the internet and find myself at the home page of a diving company. There are a couple of films on the page, one is called "Wave hit Phi Phi Island". I double click the link and lean back in the chair while waiting for the film to upload.
I can't believe my eyes. The film is shot from our hotel, over our pool!
My heart, my whole being, stops when I see what happened right where we were.
I've written and said to people that it was all silent around us...
It is certainly not silent, it's on the contrary a loud roar that I can't describe. Almost as if large aircrafts were flying towards us at low altitude.
I've heard the sound before.
I heard it when it happened, I know that now because my body recognizes the sound and reacts with full force.
My mouth is open, I don't even blink.
I just watch the movie.

First day at work

Mom is visiting us. Today is a special day, it's my first day back at work.

My first step back into the real world.

Mom makes coffee and we have breakfast together before the kids go to school and it's time for me to leave.

To be honest, I am not motivated.

My mind bubble hasn't burst yet, I'm still in the tsunami world with both body and soul.

My focus is undivided, without competition, on my children.

My body has not yet found it´s proportions – my ears are the size of elephants so that I can hear what the children say and perceive what they are not saying.

My heart is huge and red, my brain is like a hard pea and my spine is like a dinosaur, with tense nerves and muscles.

I open the door into my old world – the world I decided to say goodbye to when I was up in the jungle.

It feels like I'm in a movie. Everyone is polite, nice and well behaved in their fancy suits.

I hope my smile is as wide as it should be. I do everything I can to appear normal, but my feeling is that I come from another world. This is a world that isn't even important right now.

Maybe never again? I don't know. To be honest, I feel that I don't even have to think about the future yet. All I know is that this is not where I am supposed to be right now.

Before I leave the office, I send an email to my colleagues.
I have been in their world for half a day and I want to share a small, but important piece of my world with them.

-----Original Message-----
From: Marie-Christine Lindström
Subject: Hello again...
On December 26th at 10.35, everything changed, and much will never be the same again.

Paradise turned into a struggle for life. What couldn't happen, did happen.
The Tsunami welled in over Phi Phi Island and my family was right there, Per and I were consumed by the wave which overflooded the island in seconds. Our children watch as we disappeared into the ocean and were forced to make instant crucial decisions to save their own lives... run for their lives. How they managed to survive, I will never understand.
When you're so close to death, so close to losing your children, the world is shaking, and it hasn't stopped yet.
From the day you become a parent, you carry your heart outside your body... today I am back, and I carry my heart in my hands.
Thanks for all the flowers, phone calls and letters.
Marie

In retrospect I can see that my email was a call for help, to be able to handle the situation. See me, but don't expect too much of me. Don't pretend it's business as usual, because it's not. Nothing's like it was before. Ask me how I feel – only if you really want to hear my answer.

If you don't want to listen, don't ask anything at all, but please be nice to me.

At least for now, for a little while, until I've found myself again.

Meeting my grandmother

My grandmother, Inga, who was with me in spirit when I was in the most fearful place under the ground, has Alzheimer's and no longer knows who we are. She lives at a home for elderly in Ronneby.

The first time I visit her after the tsunami, I go to her by myself because I want to be alone with her, just as we were alone in the dark during the Tsunami.

I open the door into the ward where she lives.

I see her right away.

She sits on a couch at the end of the corridor.

My grandmother, with grey soft hair, pink cardigan and beige pants.

I get tears in my eyes as I rush over to her.

She looks up when she hears my steps.

She doesn't recognize me, I know that, but always when I get close to her, her hands start caressing my cheeks and my hair the special way she always did. Then I know that deep down, she knows who I am.

I don't say anything, I just sit close to her on the couch.

Side by side.

I take her hand in mine and put my head on her shoulder.

She starts rocking her body slowly sideways as she always used to do with me, as if to lull me calmly to settle.

I cry silently, tears fall down my cheeks as we sit there without speaking, side by side on the old couch.

She wipes away my tears with her hand.

After a while I whisper to her. "Grandma, I almost died...... I called for you..."

She says nothing, we sit in silence for a long time, her hands softly caressing my face...

I know she knows. I know she was there.

My grandmother dies exactly nine months after the Tsunami, August 26th 2005.

April 2005 - My Panic Attack

Without warning, the panic attack hits me again when I for the first time go out for a couple of drinks with the girls after the Tsunami.

The attack is triggered by the simple fact, that for a moment, I can't find them all. Is sounds strange, I know. But that is what's happened. The feelings that grabbed me and made me lose control, are similar to the feelings when I left the helicopter at Phi Phi Island. I try to escape, to go home as soon as I feel it's coming, but Anette, my best friend won't let me leave alone.

"Marie, if I was feeling the way you do now – would you have left me alone?" Her voice is firm and loud, she almost roars at me.

Something clicks. My legs don't hold me, I fall into her arms with my face over her shoulder and she grabs me the second I fall apart.

I can't hinder the sounds that pour out of me. It´s deep and primal. Screams of sadness, despair, horror, separation... all the feelings from the moment in the helicopter on Phi Phi Island that morning. It becomes so clear, that moment is the worst moment in my life. I didn't know that until right now. I have pushed down those dark feelings so deep that I didn't know they existed.

The attack goes on for a long time. My screams turn into groans, I still hyperventilate. Anette holds me tight; my knees still don't carry me. She talks to me, I don't hear what she's saying, I am just listening to her voice. She is a safe place, a familiar place.

I hear the deep screams pouring out of me and I understand that it needs to come out because it's there, but the strength scares me. I thought the panic attacks were linked to Phi Phi Island, that it would never happen here in Sweden. In the midst of the chaos during the Tsunami, everything and everyone was panicking, but on a normal Friday night in town, the attack feels so out of place and I understand that I look crazy.

We decide to go to one of our friend's place, she lives close by. I sit in the taxi near Anette and I feel her warmth, I close my eyes and concentrate on breathing. It's over now.

I'm left with a compact fatigue but also a new sense of calm. Now I know.

I understand the impact of that morning.

I also understand that this is something I need to deal with, sort out.

I can see how a panic attack is a resource, I remember the strength and energy I got at Phi Phi.

Without that panic attack, there is no way that I would have managed to make it all the way to the hospital with my family intact.

We have resources and abilities that we don't know about, that we don't usually need, but when we need that extra gear, we switch to a higher dimension to increase our presence, our decision-making skills and our physical and mental strength.

My therapist said afterwards that it's important not to avoid situations that might provoke a panic attack.

Although a panic attack feels dangerous when you are in the middle of it, it is not dangerous.

I heard his words, but I was not able to follow his advice.

For many years to come I estimate the risk before I decide to do different things.

April 17th, 2005

I pull my fingers through Anton's curly soft hair as we are
cuddled up in the coach, watching TV.
A lock of baby hair falls into his forehead, it's about 1.5 inches
long. I have noticed the same thing in mine and Axels hair. Did
we lose a lot of hair out of fear during the Tsunami and now its
growing back? `The length of the hair indicates that.
The same thing I see in my nails, I had black pieces of
'something' under my nails. As they are growing the spots are
now out by the fingertips.

April 26th, 2005

Four months, how long is that?
Sixteen weeks, sixteen Saturdays......
"Appreciate the positive things in life."
"You' did survive after all, right!"
"Be careful not to get caught up in dwelling."
"You have to move on."
So many tips...
"Appreciate the positive things in life" is a comment that
makes me frustrated.
How can anyone even for a second think that you can be in the
middle of a disaster, among dead and injured people, bring
home your entire family and not appreciate the positive things
in life? Really?
Let me make one thing extremely clear: my gratitude is so
great that it is almost religious. Does it need to be said and if
so, what words do you use? Are there even such powerful
words?

The children are outside, playing with friends. It's 3.30pm and
the laundry is hanging outside to dry in the sun.

I lie on the terrace, beautiful classical music in the stereo and the sun on my face. Sune, our dog, by my side.

My friend Anette calls to talk about the book "Conversations with God" that I got a long time ago from her but didn't start reading until today. Every sentence is full of thoughts to reflect on. "If you have this book in your hand, it's because you're supposed to read it right now, otherwise you wouldn't have it in your hand" I'm attracted to that sentence and read the first thirty pages.

We have a long conversation about life and the meaning of everything that's happening to us. And how we can learn from that.

Thank you, Anette, for being part of my life. I love you.

May 4th, 2005

Today I feel angry.
Josh Grobin's voice fills the living room where I lie on the floor.
"Fucking ocean! God damn you!!!!!"
My tears stream down my face and my chest is filled with rage.
We will never be friends again! There's no way I can forgive you for what you did, for all the children you took.
Never.
I'm going to think of you as my enemy.
The world will forgive you, but just so you know - there are many of us who will never ever forget nor forgive!
For every mother, father, or child you took there is a sadness so gigantic that we need to carry it together.

May 20th, 2005

The children and I watch the Swedish movie "As It Is In Heaven" on TV. Per is in Copenhagen with some colleagues.
We got new couches today, big and wide so we can fit all three in one coach. We are cuddled up with pillows and blankets, enjoying the movie. Those of you who have seen it, know that it is emotional, not at least at the end. When the movie's over Anton gets worried. Something is bothering him.
"I want you to call Grandpa and tell him to sleep here tonight."
"But Anton, it's 11.30pm, he is probably sleeping. And Dad will be home soon."
"I don't feel safe with you. You screamed and cried so much in Thailand." He can't stop the words. This is how he feels. It hurts me so much to see him like this. I understand what's going on with him, why he feels the way he does, and it hurts me that he still doesn't feel safe with me.
"Mom, when will I stop feeling like this?"
"Feeling like what?"

"Anxious inside? "
"It's going to get better and better but it's probably going to take some time."
"Why didn't you hug me when we met after the wave?"
We've talked about this several times; I've tried to explain what happened but it's difficult because I don't understand it myself. If it had been in a movie, our meeting would have been beautiful but now it was reality and it was chaotic and panicky. My explanation, to him and to myself, is that when I saw Per and him coming towards us, when I finally knew they were okay and alive, I handed over everything to Per, releasing all the built-up fear and pain.

If I could do one thing differently in my entire life, this is that moment I would re-do.

Anton, when we met on the ground, I would have done everything differently if I could. I would take you in my arms Anton. I would hold you tight and be the mother you needed so much right then. I would have let you rest for a while in the love I have for you, protect you from the chaos, at least for a little while.
I would have done everything so differently if only I could....

June 4th, 2005

Through the self-help POSOM group that meet weekly, I got an opportunity to get some kind of massage. I don't know much about it, just that it's a combination of therapy and massage. Something about releasing stored memories in the body.

A woman from South America meets me at the door. Her voice is low-key and soft, her hands tender, jet strong. The air is filled with scents.

We enter a large room with thin yellow curtains in the windows. Soft music fills the room.

She asks me to tell her what I've been through. When I tell her about the strong feelings that I have felt, she asks me if I can locate the feelings in my body.

"Yes, the emotions come from my left side, like a channel from my stomach and up through my throat."

"When we get to that part of your body during the massage, it's important that you breathe deeply, that you put your energy and focus right there. You need to bring those emotions to the surface so that they can be released and disappear."

I take off my clothes and sit in my underwear on a chair, she stands behind me. This is the relaxation part.

Her hands start massaging my head and my neck. My eyes are closed, and I try to relax.

Five minutes into the massage, tears are flowing down my cheeks, dripping down on my bare stomach. I wasn't prepared to feel this much, this fast.

I recognize the feeling, it's sadness.

My stomach cramps up. I can hardly breath. I can't control what's happening. After a few minutes, the crying stops just as suddenly as it started. It's so strange.

She continues to massage down my back. When her hands reach the middle of my back, a cramp comes right there, I'm gasping for air.

"My back hurts."

"Here?" She puts her hand on a spot on my back.

"A little further down."
The cramp gets worse when she finds the right place. I can hardly breathe.
Tears are flowing again, uncontrollably. She tries to help me breathe, to take deep breaths.
I hear her breathing behind me, and I follow into her breathing rhythm. We breath together, from the deepest parts of my body. At the end I release a loud exhale, almost like a quiet scream.
My body becomes calm again and the exercise is finished. She asks me to lie down on my stomach. I get some paper napkins and wipe off my wet face before I turn around on the bench. She puts big soft towels over me and starts massaging my right foot and continues up my leg. I have some tension in my calf, she asks me to breathe deeply.
The towel is moved down and she gently puts her warm hands on my scarred spine and back.
As on a signal from above, my tears start flowing again, with such force that I barely get any air. She keeps one hand over my spine and the other one on the middle of my back. She just stands still and lets my emotions flow. My stomach clenches in cramps when the emotions are peaking. A mountain of stormy emotions is to be climbed. On the way down from the top, slowly the crying begins to give in. My nose is blocked, she reaches for a napkin so I can blow my nose and wipe my face. The massage continues up to the neck and out towards my right arm and hand. When she reaches my left arm, my skin stings as if I had burned myself in the sun. I turn over to lie on my back. My eyes have been closed since we started, I have a hard time opening them.
She is moving her hands above my body; I feel the heat. When she puts her hands along the left side of my stomach, where I told her my channel is, tears start flowing again. She puts her hands on the opposite side of my stomach, and the tears stops. After a while, I don't know from where, but I hear it clearly, someone saying out loud: "You were meant to die in Thailand".
I know she's not saying anything, I know I'm not thinking it, so where did it come from?

"I just heard that I was meant to die Thailand." I feel that I must tell her. She does not respond; she just keeps on massaging.

After another ten minutes we are finished, I get a glass of water and a napkin to wipe my eyes with.

"Have you had pain in your back after the Tsunami?"

"Yes, and my chiropractor has not been able to help me. He says that right there in the middle, the muscles are completely tense, he can't do anything about it.

I haven't been able to lie down on the floor because it feels like the spine is concave, that there's a bump in my back. I've always had some problems with my back, so I know my back very well. This is completely different from anything I ever felt before. They even did an x-ray and that didn't reveal any injuries. "

She is nodding. "You see, the shocking emotions got stuck in your back."

I look at her and I know right away that she is right. That's why I couldn't put into words what I felt and that's why the x-ray didn't show anything.

"When I placed my hands on your spine where you had a lot of injuries, the energy and power were so strong."

Everything she says makes so much sense to me.

My body remembers the moments that I am not aware of.

The moments when I might not even have been conscious, the moments when I got all my injuries.

She continues to talk about how the spine follows life. When something terrible happens, it shows in the back. That is why if you do not address strong emotions, they will manifest in psychosomatic diseases, often located in the back.

She continues." You were divided in the middle, Marie."

I leave her with the most amazing feeling of liberation.

June 15th, 2005

I receive a letter from the police that my passport has arrived at the police station in Malmo. I tremble as I read it.
I handed in my passport as a "deposit" at the hotel at Phi Phi on December 24th when we checked in. They stored it in their archives, which was below sea level. I never thought I'd get it back.

When I get my passport in my hand it´s rough and salty.
When I turn the sides, there is sand and salt between the sides.

The hidden room

I'm not a therapist, but now I know what it feels like, at least in my brain, when you're in lethal danger.
This is how I see it:
Imagine you're looking at your brain from above. You see four different rooms, one at the front along the entire forehead, one at the back of the neck and two along the sides of the brain.
Normally we use the two side parts. This is where we worry, find solutions, make notes that we need to buy milk and bread.
When there is chaos and you fight for your life, all the activity in the brain goes straight to the front of the forehead and everything happens from now on in that room – the hidden room.
In that room, all thoughts are stripped down, and you function as I imagine a soldier does in war.
There's no place for emotions in that room. Or doubt.
You make decisions without spending much time weighing pros and cons.
We don't know what it's like to be in that hidden room as we don't need to under normal circumstances.
I now see that room as my friend. My friend for life.

It was safe to be there, without too many feelings or insights. To have the ability to disconnect in order to be able to act. The fear didn't go away, probably because it is the fuel that kicks open the door to the hidden room where we need to go to survive.

Your hearing becomes incredibly intense, you hear EVERYTHING that needs to be heard as if your brain helps the ears to select in a way you didn't know was possible. All the unimportant sounds are deselected, and the important sounds are amplified.

The hidden room also affects you vision. You see everything as through a tunnel. There is no wide angle, the head is moving instead. You view feet by feet. You see what needs to be seen. The awareness is huge!

All the vital senses, hearing, vision, and the ability to make decisions and execute them... everything is done with the utmost focus.
I actually feel what it's like, just writing about it.
Once you have been in your hidden room, you can probably always find it again and that's good...and bad.
I wonder if it's not in the hidden room that panic attacks can start again precisely because the door is partly open and it's in that room you store memories and feelings that you haven't addressed. You may not even remember everything, but subconsciously, it's still there.

When we got home, I was afraid to go to bed because I was frightened that memories from the wave would come back.
I was terrified thinking about my struggle in the wave, down in the dark water.
In my conscious memories, I'm unconscious when I am in the wave, but what if I wasn't? Would I really have survived if I had been unconscious? What if I completely blocked my memories because I don't dare to remember?

I certainly didn't want to remember anything more right now so every time I felt that my brain was approaching something that could be memories of the struggle in the water, I twisted my head fast from side to side, to make it stop.
It worked.

The job interview

When we were up in the jungle, I decided it's enough for me working fifty- sixty hours a week. It is not worth it even if it shows in the paycheck. That's not how I want to live my life any longer.

I kept my eyes open for another job and one day I saw it in the newspaper. The largest bank in the Nordic region were looking for investment and insurance specialists. I knew right away that this is the job for me.

Two weeks later I get a call from the bank. They want to see me.

With butterflies in my stomach, I meet the man who came to be my boss. One of the best I've ever had. The interview went like most job interviews – I was nervous and tense, but everything felt good. Until he asked me:

"What is your work situation today? Can you please describe a usual working day?"

I can't lie. I can't do that. He has the right to know.

"So, right now I'm only working part time. We were in the Tsunami and since then I've been home on sick leave. First full-time and now at part-time..."

His eyes change, he swallows and looks down. He doesn't know what to say. I'm thinking he will never hire me after this. After a minute or two he asks: "Did everyone make it?"

"Yes, everyone made it."

When I leave the room, I'm convinced that I won't get the job. Who would dare hire me? A mother with a sore and vulnerable heart?

A few days later a got a call. I got the job! I got it!

The promises I made to myself, up in the jungle were sacred and it was important to implement everything I had decided. I saw it as an obligation, to myself and to Anton and Axel.

Another part of my mission was completed.

The return to Thailand

The closer we get to the anniversary of the Tsunami, the more I fear it.
What do we do that day?
Celebrate life?
But what about all those who didn't make it?

Since I was injured and hospitalized in Thailand, I'm part of a group that is invited to a memorial service in Thailand on the anniversary. But all I want is to be with my family that day so that option is unthinkable.
One day at work, at the end of November, I see by chance a travel ad in the newspaper.
It's a last-minute travel, only air fare, one week to Phuket. There are five seats left.
I call Per at work and convince him that we need to go back. After a while he agrees, and I call the travel company and book four tickets.

The children need new passports and we need to be vaccinated so we are busy arranging everything before the trip.
This is not a trip anyone look forward to. But it's a trip we need to make. I just know that in my gut. If something scares you this much, you need to face it to overcome the fear. To be able to heal and move on.
And we can't do this later, right now is the time. I have seen on the Internet that Phi Phi Island is still completely destroyed, and I know that reconstruction has begun. If we wait for one or two more years there will be tourists around the pool at our hotel, drinking drinks and having fun. It would be a completely unreal and conflicting sight. I want us to go there now, while it still looks like a mess so we can get clarity on each other's paths and stories. I want us to go there now to understand that it did happen. I want us to see the misery and I am convinced that it is the right thing for the children, otherwise I would never put them through this.

Through a website I received information about TVAI, a volunteer organization, which help people on site. The volunteers are persons who normally work as therapists, nurses and other roles within health care. TVAI is cooperating with the Emergency Services and the Swedish Church on site. TVAI is located at a Swedish-owned hotel that survived the Tsunami and where you can book rooms via the organization. I email TVAI and get in touch with a helpful woman. '
We communicate back and forth for a few days. Booking rooms, arranging for her to pick us up at the airport etc. The questions are many. What flight do you arrive on, how old are the children, where were you during the Tsunami, what places do you want to visit?

I let her know that I lost myself in the chaos and when we return this time, I really need to show my children that they can trust me. That I am still the mother they knew. The mother they always had.
Under no circumstances must I lose control on the island!!!
If I do, the journey will have the opposite effect.
When I lie in bed in the dark, the scenario always looks the same: the boat comes ashore, I take a few steps up on the island, walk up to a palm tree, put an arm around the tree and throw up.
I let her know that I really need some help to prevent that from happening.
We make a plan together.
She's amazing.
We decide that we are going to Phi Phi Island together with a person from the Swedish Rescue Service and a priest from the Swedish Church.
She gives me the contact information to the Swedish Rescue Service, and I ask them the questions that I have spinning in my head: do you have walkie talkies? If there is another expected earthquake while we are on the island, will you know that right away? Can we be safe during the time we are on the island so that we can focus on why we are there?

We decide to visit Phi Phi our first day in Thailand. We are going to arrive late in the afternoon, they will pick us up and we are going directly to the hotel to get an early night's sleep. The Rescue Service and the priest come and pick us up at the hotel at 7am, the morning after.

Are you sure you want to go to Phi Phi on your first day? Isn't it better to wait a day or two?

No, it's not better to wait. Going there is the worst thing I have ever asked my children to do. I force them to return to the place on earth where both stood alone, convinced that the rest of the family is dead. That they were all alone in the world. For Anton & Axel this is hell on earth and who wants to go to such a place?

There is not a lot of packing that needs to be done. It's mostly our minds we need to prepare, each of us in our own way. I can actually feel how everyone is preparing, it's a tension in the air you can almost touch. We don't talk much, but we reflect all the more.

I talk to Marianne at the Red Cross who is in charge of my POSOM group. She starts crying when I tell her we are going back to Phi Phi Island.

"It's the right thing to do, Marie. I know you need to do this, and I am absolutely convinced that you will leave Thailand stronger, more healed and, above all, not as afraid."

I tell her about the unwanted scene that's stuck in my mind; me vomiting by a palm tree.

"You have to gather all the power you have, mobilize your entire inner Marie. You can't lose control on the island. Focus on the kids and call me whenever you want and need, Marie!"

Phi Phi Island and the hospital

I don't remember much of the drive to the airport.
I am fully concentrated and focused on what we have in front
of us. Last time we left for Thailand was with excitement and
anticipation, now we have a serious task ahead of us.
We are not the only Tsunami victims at the airport as the
anniversary is approaching.
We fly directly to Phuket, the airport we left from after the
Tsunami.

As we enter the airport the scent of Thailand mixes with the
humid air, I breathe deeply and my heart beats fast.
Boom, boom, boom, boom...
My throat feels tight, I swallow.
I turn my head back and forth from right to left, right to left.
The ocean is close to the runways, the ground is flat, no hills or
mountains that can protect. I remember the rumors from the
jungle: Phuket airport is under water; all the planes have
disappeared.
I force myself to swallow; I look at the children.
Their faces are pale, their eyes overlook the ocean the same
way I particularly remember Anton was doing the last time we
were here.
We head for the exit; I hold Axel in one hand and Anton in the
other.

The doors open and there are two women from TVAI waiting
for us. It so nice to see their shirts with the TVAI sign. It brings
a feeling of security. I know they have direct contact with the
Rescue Service and if there had been an earthquake, they
would know about it.
The fact that the risk that a new earthquake would occur again
is highly unlikely, does not matter.

The hotel is located a short distance from the ocean, about 820 feet, and is set on a hill. The woman next to me tells me that the wave hit here too but didn't go further than halfway up to the hotel. I shudder in the heat. I can picture the grey water welling up over the lawn.

I get a call from the Rescue Service. They just want to check that everything is okay for tomorrow. He repeats our schedule: At 7am sharp they will be waiting for us in the reception and it takes almost 90 minutes to go to the pier from where the boat to Phi Phi leaves.

I appreciate that he calls me to check in. I tell them that we are nervous. His voice is calm and stable.

We eat dinner and for a while we are just present, here and now, with each other, and for a while we forget about tomorrow.

We go to bed all four of us at 9 pm. Just as we are about to fall asleep, the sky lights up with fireworks. Both me and the children get terrified by the sudden sound.

It turns out it's the celebration of the King of Thailand, it's his birthday. If only we had known, we would not be so scared by the sudden sound. After that, we have a hard time to settle down with all the adrenaline pumping in our bodies.

The children and Per eventually fall asleep, I lay awake with my own thoughts.

I must make it through tomorrow, I have to be strong, I have to be reliable. If I feel the panic coming, I need to walk away, call someone.

I cannot vomit by a tree.

I need to be good, be strong, not behave like I did the 26th.

I need to prove to my children that they can trust me.

We wake up at quarter to six in the morning. We put on the clothes that we prepared bedtime yesterday and go down to the restaurant.

I look at the children as they sit around the table.

Their eyes are like glass.

It's hard to reach them, to get any contact with them.

I leave for the reception in advance so that I can get a few minutes by myself with our two heroes waiting for us.
I see them straight away. The man from the Rescue Service is tall and shaved on his head. He looks at me with a warm smile. The priest is a little shorter, also with a warm smile. I instantly get a safe good feeling. I'll tell them about my children, that they are having a hard time. That I'm having a hard time. That I need their help to keep an extra eye on Anton and Axel.
I do not really know what I'm asking them to do, I just need to let them know that I am a terrified mother with equally frightened children.

Anton, Axel and Per come up to us. They greet in a polite way. Every muscle is tense in their bodies and faces.
Am I out of my mind? What the hell am I doing? How can I force my children to do this? Isn't it enough with what they already have been through? Now I force them to go there AGAIN??
My thoughts are spinning, if I could have done everything differently right now, I would have been home, watching them play ice hockey, as all their friends are doing, instead of forcing them to be here!
Is this really the right thing to do??
What if it gets worse??
If only there had been a manual – "This is how you deal with traumatized children. A book for traumatized parents."
Is there such a book?
If not, why not?
Some things in life you only get one chance to do right.
If you make mistakes, the opportunity is gone.
And who is going to pay the price for that mistake?
The child who's going to live with the consequences for the rest of his life. That is exactly how it feels right now, right here.
Marie, it's time for you to prove how good of a mom you are!
Are you making the right decisions? The right actions?
The pressure I put on myself is heavy to carry.

We get into their big Van and the journey towards Phi Phi Island begins.

They make sure the conversation during the car ride flows easily. We even laugh a little. I can see that the children relax a little, and so do I.

The car slows down, and we approach the pier.

"Marie, this is where we came ashore with the boat after the Tsunami. Over there the boat docked, and this is where the ambulances were waiting. Do you remember?" Per is pointing with his hand, he speaks fast, with a strained voice.

My body gets tense and hard. I don't recognize myself at first, I need to search hard through my memories. I was sure I had thought about everything, prepared myself for everything but I completely forgot about this. Forgot how and where we came ashore from Phi Phi.

The memories begin to play, like a movie in my mind.

Per keeps talking. "You may not recognize this place because that day, there were lots of people and ambulances everywhere."

Slowly I start to remember. It looks so different now, almost empty, just a couple of Japanese tourists.

"Do you remember that they put you on a stretcher and that the ambulance was too close to a high curb? So the ambulance had to drive up a little bit and they told you not to get scared when the stretcher tilted down the edge? Do you remember that?"

If I remember?

Yes...

I remember the feeling of the hard grip around my arms as we walked from the boat towards the ambulance, the stretcher towards my body, the face of the nurse who was talking to me....

I just don't remember what it looked like around me.

The only thing I focused on was your faces.

I needed to see the three of you.

I was so afraid to lose you in the crowd, afraid that you wouldn't be able to follow me as everything was happening so suddenly and fast.

Our car stops and we walk towards the building. The ground is paved in grey stones. The sidewalk edge is high, I see that now and I remember how the stretcher fell, how the metal crashed. As we walk towards the boat I remember all the Thais that were handing out food to everyone who came from Phi Phi, transparent plastic bags of rice and chicken. How on earth did they have time to prepare everything? There were so many of us and there was food and water bottles for all of us.

The sun is shining on us as we slowly board the boat that will take us to Phi Phi.

The boat trip takes about 90 minutes and all four of us escape deeply into our own thoughts, we don't speak a lot.

As we approach Phi Phi, my body starts to prepare for what's coming. Now it's time, time to gather the power I need to carry out the mission we have in front of us. I'm starting to feel sick, nervous, sweaty. The kids are watching me to see what I behave like, to see if they can rely on their mother.

We are standing by the taffrail and I begin to talk to them while we are looking at the island as we are getting closer and closer.

The island is completely bare. Naked. You can see over to the bay on the other side of the island.

We approach a pier just in front of Phi Phi Island Cabana hotel.

The air is warm. It's quiet, far from the ecstasy the 27th when we left the island.

I see that Anton looks very nervous.

And that same second, I realize that I am calm and focused... Thank God.

I'm calm.

I'm not going to throw up by a tree.

I'm going to be a good mom here on the island.

I'm going to get through this. I know that now.

I am going to be able to help Anton and Axel, focus on them. The only thing that matters here and now.

I walk across the pier and put my feet on Phi Phi. And it feels okay.

Anton has told me that he does not want to go to the tennis court where the helicopters were, but somehow that's exactly what's happening.
I see Anton's head going back and forth. How he looks over to the patch of grass where he and Axel were left all alone by Per and me that horrible morning.
This is where he went through hell on earth.
I see that. It's obvious.
Big brother, 11 years old, with his younger brother by his side. All alone.
Dad's picking up injured people in the village and mom's leaving with a helicopter without anyone knowing where she´s going. Only that she is injured.
He must have been so afraid.
He starts talking. About the longtail boat that crashed towards the hotel.
His arms are swinging back and forth, he's not still for a single second.
I walk by his side and listen to him.
I try not to touch him; he is so restless that he doesn't want any physical contact. I see that so I just try to be close to him with my presence and awareness.
Axel, on the other hand, has difficulty navigating himself, difficult to understand where we are and where everything is. He doesn't even remember where the pool is.
He wants me to hold his hand. He is in a better place than Anton. He was so much younger. I remember that when it became clear to him that we were all alive, I could see that he begun to heal.
Anton, being older, understood the gravity of what happened.

It feels so good to have our two companions by our side. I see how they have full control over how the four of us are doing. We walk around our hotel and arrive at the pool area. My heart beats hard in my chest.
This is where it all happened.

It looks like a construction site. The fountain is covered with blue canvas and some people are on their knees, replacing damaged tiles on the ground. The entire pool area looks awful. A metal ladder from the pool is removed and put aside. It's completely twisted, as if a big boat had hit it.

The power of the Tsunami is obvious. I slowly walk towards the very spot where I stood when I started to look out over the bay.

Per comes close to me.

We stand there for a while in silence. It´s still so hard to grasp. Axel takes my hand; I turn around and look at Anton. He walks by himself on the other side of the pool, with his arms wavering back and forth...

I walk over to him and ask him questions about where he stood, what it looked like.

He tells me that he stood by himself when all the adults ran away and that he tried to shout to Per and me that we should run, that we should hurry to get away from here. He tells me that the wave was higher than the palm trees the last time he looked out at the ocean before the wave hit.

He tells me that he saw when the Tsunami took Per and me. And after that he ran for his life, up towards the hotel, around a corner. That's where the wave caught up with him and hit him in the back with such force that he went straight ahead to the stairway where his arm got stuck.

We follow the path he describes and around a corner is the green stair rail he is talking about.

That stair rail probably saved his life as he got stuck and therefore wasn't dragged away in the wave.

He is somehow managing to mobilize the force to pull himself up from the ocean and rush up the stairs.

We are following his path while we are talking. At home he has tried to describe the path, but we have not understood what he meant.

Now that we are here, I see that he found the fastest smartest way to get as high as possible.

He talks fast and he walks fast.

We reach the restaurant level.

He shows me where he climbed a table to reach the roof. He tells me that some Thai men pulled him by his long hair to get past him up on the roof. Somehow, he managed to hold on and climb his way up to the roof.

On the roof he walks around and around. A man comes up to him and ask him where his mother and father is.

"I have lost my mother, father and brother", Anton responds in English. He borrows the man's cell phone to call grandma or grandpa.

Anton doesn't know that you need to dial an international country code, so he doesn't reach anyone.

I ask him what he is thinking while he is up here by himself. He says he´s thinking about where he's going to live and how is it going to be with all his food allergies, and who's going to take him to his ice hockey.

There was a small boy swimming in the pool next to Anton just before the wave came, Anton sees a man coming carrying the boy in his arm.

The boy is shattered and dead.

I look at his face as he talks. He does everything he can to appear grown-up instead of sad or scared.

You can tell by his face and eyes that he was so scared up here, that he wasn't even sad, that he couldn't even cry.

Then the Dutchman who was on the diving boat the day before came up to Anton and said that he has seen Per, that Per is on the other side of the roof. Anton starts running and there, around a corner on the roof they meet.

Anton and Per.

Anton was no longer alone and Per told him that he heard me shouting before so he knew I had survived. But they didn't know anything about Axel yet.

It will be another three more hours before we all meet.

While we walk around, a Thai girl comes up to us. She points at a Thai man and says that he recognizes Anton from the tsunami, that he and Anton ran next to each other. The man comes up to us and when he hears that we want to get up on the roof he assists us so that Per, Anton and Axel can climb up. Per is filming on the roof with the video camera.

When I watch the video later, it's obvious how strong the emotions were between Per and Anton on that roof.

In the film Per is repeating over and over: "And this is where Anton and I met... here I met Anton... here, Anton and I met."

After the roof we head back to the ground in our search for everyone's path.

Down by the pool we walk over to the stairs that leads under the hotel. Down to the basement where Per and I ended up in the wave.

Slowly we walk down the stairs, towards the dark basement. Anton hurries down to see what it looks like.

Axel steps on broken tiles to hear how it sounds when they break.

As I walk down the stairs, it feels like someone grabs me by my throat and holds tight. So tight that I have trouble inhaling the damp scent. Fear and memories join me as I set foot underground.

They have cleaned up some of the debris. I see the beams on the ceiling that I only felt with my hands but never saw with my eyes because it was so black when I was here. It looks exactly as I described it.

There are large rectangular holes in the walls, close to the ceiling. That's where the air-conditions was before the wave pulled them away.

Per continues to talk into the camera. I hear him say that he ended up climbing out through one of these holes. He says that as he heard the water pouring but he did not know if it was pouring in or out so he shoved his hand into a sharp nail on the wall to keep his hand still. He touched his fingertips, the water lever, the fingertips again to figure out if the level went up or down. As the water slowly, slowly sank away after a while, he began to get a glimpse of light and he began to swim that way. Somehow, he managed to crawl out through a narrow hole.

He doesn't know where he went after that or how he got up on the roof.

We stay down in the basement for a while, Anton goes back and forth.

He is thinking, reflecting.

And we just let him do what he needs to do.

Axel wants to go up. He wants to show us his path.

I take his hand in mine and we walk up the stairs, out on the pool area again. Per and Anton stay for a while in the underground.

Axel starts telling me that he comes walking on the little path from our hotel room. He has a ball in one hand and the towel for me in the other along with the plastic key to our room. As he approaches the pool he sees it, the wave or rather, the wall of water coming his way. Its higher than the palm trees. He sees Anton next to the pool. He screams as loud as he can to Anton and then he turns around and starts running.

He runs the fastest he can until he comes to a curve where he collides with a man and falls straight into the bushes. The ball falls out of his hand. The man stops, turns back, and helps Axel up on his feet again.

He starts running again, as fast as he can to our hotel building, up the stairs to our room. He opens the door to our room and runs up to the panoramic window overlooking the bay.

The black wall of water is at the window. He gets so scared that he runs out of the room, out into the loft aisle.

The water comes up to the floor just beneath Axel. He stands there looking out over the island that by now is below sea level.

He sees a man in the wave, desperately trying to stay alive by holding on to a branch.

Axel will not tell me what happened next to that man, He´s not sure what he's seen.

He bites at the plastic key to our room as he stands here looking out over the island. We have that room key at home, with his small bite marks all over it.

A man asks him something in English. But Axel doesn't speak English. He's only eight years old.

I ask him what he is thinking about when he is standing there. He thinks that he cannot talk to anyone here, no one understands Swedish, so no one can help him to come home again. Ever.

He's going to have to stay here, by himself, forever.

The water sinks away after a while and Axel stands there with
the man by his side. He looks down and sees me coming.
He is shocked because he was so sure that we had all died in
the wave.
We walk along the aisle outside our room while Axel describes
what happened and what he was thinking.
We go step by step, follow the same paths we ran eleven
months ago.
Every step is a long, important step.
When we have walked everyone's different paths at the hotel,
we walk over to the jungle. It´s not a nice jungle. It's tricky and
nasty. It's easy to imagine snakes and other insects here. But
that night it was paradise on earth. The only place we felt safe
here at Phi Phi.

Later that afternoon we have a coffee at a small bar before
leaving the island. Anton and Per have been down in the
basement once again. It's obvious that he needed to come back
here to see it all again.
The priest whispers to me: "Anton is not the same person he
was when we picked you up this morning, it's like turning a
hand. It's amazing to see. You really did a good thing, coming
back here. Even if it was a challenge, you can see how
necessary it is to return and close the circle."
We leave Phi Phi Island, standing together in the back of the
boat, watching the island get smaller and smaller.
And we are good.

Returning to the hospital

The next day we go to the hospital together with one of the volunteers. We want to see our room again and I hope to meet some of the people who took such good care of us. To thank them.

The car stops outside the emergency room where we came with the ambulance. I remember everything in detail. We look into the emergency room, I see where they put me and my stretcher. I remember how the pain was turned on as soon as the stretcher stopped by the wall and the staff started to work on my injuries.

I also remember the feeling of one step of the mission completed, and the relief that we no longer need to be terrified.

A nurse shows us the way to a room. She knocks on the door and we step in.

There is my doctor. His gentle eyes light up when he sees us. I take his hand between my two and find it difficult to talk. I remember the security I felt as soon as he was near me. I had such confidence in him.

The word Thank you is so small in relation to what he did for me, for us.

On the way up to our room, we meet the nurse who had the main responsibility for me. She lights up when she sees us, and she hugs my hands. The volunteer who is with us ask me if I would like to know what is in my medical records. The nurse goes and picks them up.

Her English isn't very good, but I understand that I had lost a lot of blood and that I was very affected by my injuries when I came to the hospital.

She shows us the way to our room. There is a patient in bed, but we get permission to go in quietly. The room looks exactly the way I remember it.

I want to see the bathroom, we go in and when I see the light blue sink, I get touched.

Maybe because it was in here, I saw my wounded body?
Because this is where Per washed my hair, and we placed all
the stuff from my hair and head on the sink?
We end the visit to the hospital with the children showing me
the store where they bought their food during our stay her.
Before leaving, we enjoyed a freshly squeezed orange juice in
plastic bags with inserted straw.

During the car ride back to the hotel I feel that we have closed
the circle. It feels so good.
Now I would have liked to return home, to Sweden, but we still
have a few more days before the flight goes home.
We spend the time shopping and by the pool.
Until the last day.
Per wants us to go down to the beach, to the ocean.
I don't want to but he whispers to me that it is important to
show the children they can swim and play in the ocean just as
they did before the Tsunami.
I know that he is right.
We head for the beach, my steps are hesitant and slow.
I put our towel out and I sit in the sand with my back straight
and my eyes gazing out over the sea.
I don't dare to lie down or close my eyes. The children are at
first a little careful, but after a short while they behave as
usual. They jump and splash, dive and laugh.
They start to dig a hole in the sand.
With their backs facing the ocean. I look at them and think
that I could never have dreamed of them feeling so safe so fast.
Per takes a photo of them, the children kneeling in the sand,
backs towards the sea and behind them a wave that strikes.
A sign that we have moved on.
And the most important thing of all - the children have begun
to heal.

December 2005

I have written about our return trip, but I still don't want to read it myself.

The words have poured out from within. The same day that the children went to school after the Christmas break 2004-2005, I sat down at the computer and let everything flow. I needed to get it out and I wanted to give my children some kind of explanation for everything strange that happened at Phi Phi Island. Not that I understand everything, or can explain everything, but I wanted to give them what I can give them and that is my story.

It's not fancy or beautiful because that not what it was like. But I hope I have managed to put some words on the unexplainable in the attempt of sharing what was happening inside me, why I became so different and at times even frightening.

I want to give them an insight, maybe not for now when they still are young, but for later in their lives, about the chaos within me.

My intellect was at war with my feelings. I made a mistake - I let the intellect take over when I should have followed my feelings, I will never do that again.

For now, we are doing fine, as a family.

And with my heart filled of gratitude I can honestly say that I have never felt as alive as I do now.

Five years later

I'm reading my story for the first time since I wrote it.
I don't really understand that these are my words.
There is wisdom and nudity that I do not recognize.
I'm very happy that I wrote down everything as soon as we
came home, because today I would not have been able to write
my story. Time has erased the sharpest edges from the
experience, softened the worst fears and placed a protective
layer over the nudity to fit into the world.
Reading what I wrote during the afternoons while my children
were at school, I get pulled back into the memories.
I re-live the pain, the love, the joy and the fears.

Today we are still talking about what happened at least once a
month.
As for Axel, I notice that when he starts in a new school or
class, he shares "his story" as he calls it, both for the
headmaster, the children, and the teacher. It's like he needs to
put his story out there and then he can go on living his life.
Anton is in the middle of the teen phase, so he doesn't talk
much about how he feels right now. He often mentions
something briefly but then clearly shows that he doesn't want
me to "dwell" on it. He is very protective of his brother. And he
is always on his guard.

I am stronger and angrier and happier. My fear of feeling fear
is still strong and it's probably something I will have to work
with for the rest of my life.
I live life fast, with my heart as a compass and always try to
follow my intuition and inner voice.
I enjoy life more than ever before.

Per lives more in the present. And he is very protective of us.
Together we have become stronger as a couple.
We did not separate as I was afraid of.

As a family, much has changed around us lately. The first years after the Tsunami we lived in a bubble, close together, the four of us.
Today I would say our lives are more normal, but we are still close.
I can see situations and decisions that have been made entirely based on what we were through.
I am still a tigress as a mother.
There is nothing I would not do to protect Anton and Axel.
If I need to go to the end of the world for them, I will.
Nothing will ever be more important.

September 2013

Almost nine years. Nine years!
It feels like yesterday and at the same time like an eternity has passed.
When I read the story that slowly is becoming a book, I am moved. When I read about how the kids were doing, what they went through, what they saw. When I read about being in the wave and ending up underground, I still get terrified.

The man who saved my life is in my mind more and more often.
Who is he?
What kind of person takes an active choice to risk his own life to save mine?
A person completely unknown to him?
I would love to meet him.

We talk about the Tsunami more often today than we did four or five years ago, often at the initiative of the children. Maybe because they are older? Seventeen and twenty years old. Small boys have become two young men. No matter why they choose to talk about the Tsunami, I'm glad they do. Glad that together we created a platform without limitations, without timeframes.
The more I heard words about not getting caught up in dwelling, the more I told my children to never let anyone else decide when and how you process things you have been through. There are no rules to follow. It's your feelings, your thoughts, and you're in charge.
What the children bring up today is completely different things than what we talked about when they were younger, and I guess that's how it is going to be.
I often get the question how we live differently today, after the tsunami, and that question is difficult to answer. I don't know what our life would have been like if it had not happened.

And the children were young. We have daily close contact, but we probably would have had that anyway.

Anton and Axel are very close.

I see that, I love that.

The four of us share the desire to get the best out of life.

I am mostly happy, but of course I wake up sometimes not feeling great. But I know that I have the power to influence my day and my life in the direction I choose.

I am often grateful that I got a chance to continue to walk this road called life.

With perspective, I still feel strongly about the way society divided us into groups based on death/no death. The actual death, not the experience or fear of death. As I wrote at the beginning of the book, survivors often feel guilty . This combined with the fact that society so clearly showed that death was a divider in terms of the support you got, that was not good.

I would have wanted my children, who thought everyone else was dead, to get qualified help.

I googled children and traumatic events in January 2005 and found an article about the difference in children's health regarding those affected on the 11th of September in US. Children that received quick and adequate help felt much better than those who didn't. Today, many years later, natural disasters are reasons for qualified help in Sweden.

Axel asked me a few months ago " Mom, do you remember anything from the time before the tsunami?" at first, I did not understand the question, of course I remember, I was 40 years old. But after thinking for a while, I sensed what he meant. There is a before and a after.

"What about you Axel?"

"I remember almost nothing from before the Tsunami. It's like my life started afterwards," he says, looking at me with his young wise eyes.

"I'm not afraid of anything because the worst has already happened," says the woman in the interview on tv.

I'm scared, Anton and Axel.
Afraid of losing you two.
It's the worst thing that could happen.
I swam in the sea of losing you and I never want to get near
that again. It was hell on earth.
I'm your mother, the mother you know so well.
 I'm not the mother you saw at Phi Phi Island, and you know
that now.
Never hesitate.
I'm here for you.
Up to the moon and back.
Always and forever.

November 2020

So, it´s time to let go.
Let this book find those that might find comfort, recognition
or inspiration.
We are only human.
We do the best we can.
I feel sad when I think about all the guilt I carried around.
Guilt and remorse of not being enough. Of not being a good
mother. Of surviving.
I searched for stories that would make me feel better, make me
feel normal.
But I didn't find any.
The best thing I could ever wish for with this book is exactly
that – that my words, my naked, sometimes unpleasant, story,
might help someone to feel that its ok to be human.

We do our best and with love as our ground and foundation, it
will be okay in the end.

With Love,
Marie

The end

SYDSVENSKA DAGBLADET SNÄLLPOSTEN ≡ GRUNDAD 1848 ≡ SYDSVENSKAN.SE

SYDSVENSKAN

SÖNDAG
2 JANUARI 2005 +4
≡ Vecka 53 ≡ Årgång 157 ≡ Nr 1 ≡ Pris 15 kr

Per T Ohlsson: »I sökandet efter den stora tryggheten
började vi förtränga hoten och riskerna.«

Opinion A5

Katastrofen i Sydostasien: Hela familjen på väg hem

FOTO: LEIF R ANDERSSON

Familjen Lindström från Malmö drabbades av katastrofen på Phi Phi-öarna. Som genom ett mirakel skadades bara Marie, registrerad som nummer 204
av de skadade svenskarna i Phuket. Här är familjen återförenad på Phukets flygplats. Axel, Marie, Anton och i bakgrunden pappa Per.

Nummer 204 får resa hem

▶ När flodvågen rullade in över Phi Phi-
öarna befann sig Marie Lindström vid
barnpoolen på hotellet. Medan hennes
båda söner sökte skydd från vattenmas-
sorna uppe i hotellet kastades hon och
hennes man Per runt i de kraftiga virv-

larna. Nästa minne Marie Lindström kan
berätta för Sydsvenskans utsända i Thailand är att hon är i en avloppstrumma under poolen, skadad i höften.

Nummer 204 är registreringen från
sjukhuset, kvittot på att Marie Lind-

ström var stark nog att klara av hemre-
san till Sverige och Malmö. På planet
fick hon sällskap av sin familj.

Phukets flygplats är ett gytter av pati-
enter, vårdpersonal, journalister och vo-
lontärer. Sedan den svenska luftbron

öppnades har allt flutit smidigt trots
kaos på ytan. Regelverket har ställts åt
sidan för mänskliga hänsyn.

Men ännu är det inte säkert att alla
skadade svenskar verkligen har hämrats
ut från sjukhusen.

3 559 saknade

3 559 svenskar saknas fortfarande i Asien enligt UD, de fles-
ta i Thailand. Men siffran är
fortfarande mycket osäker. Sa-
knade hittas hela tiden, men
samtidigt läggs nya namn till
listan över försvunna.

En sorgens dag

Första dagen på det nya året var
en nationell sorgedag. Flaggorna
utanför Lunds domkyrka vajade
på halv stång liksom på många
andra platser.
Kyrkan var fylld av folk och av
levande ljus.

»Överlevande känner skuld
över att de överlevt.
Oskadda över att de inte
skadats. De som fått hjälp
över att andra inte fått det.«

Sydsvenskans **Karen Söderberg** om katastrofen.

Kinesisk hjälp

Den svenska identifieringskom-
missionen stannar i Thailand
till dess alla döda är identifiera-
de.
I arbetet med att fastställa de
avlidnas identiteter får gruppen
hjälp bland annat från Kina.

Katastrofen i Sydostasien A6–A12. Opinion A4–A5. Kultur B4–B5, Lund C6–C7, Omkretsen C12, Söndag D1–D9. Följ utvecklingen på Sydsvenskan.se

Bonus material - Questions for reflection and discussion

For you personally, together with a friend
or in your **Book Club**

1. What three words would you use to describe the book?
2. Are there parts of the book you are still thinking about?
3. Has this book affected the way you look at your life? If so, in what way?
4. What are the passages that particularly affected you?
5. What is the most important point the author makes in this book?
6. What was your favourite part of the book?
7. Did you race to the end, or was it more of a slow burn?
8. Which scene has stuck with you the most?
9. Did you reread any passages? If so, which ones?
10. Did reading the book impact your mood? If yes, how so?
11. What surprised you most about the book?
12. If you could ask the author anything, what would it be?
13. Do you think you will remember this book in a few months? If so, in what way?
14. Who do you most want to read this book?

Make sure to follow for book deals and upcoming book releases.

marielindstrom.com

Printed in Great Britain
by Amazon

73771707R00119